D0324328

The Gazette Girls
of Grundy County

FV

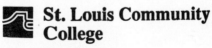

St. Louis Community College

Forest Park
Florissant Valley
Meramec

Instructional Resources
St. Louis, Missouri

GAYLORD

The Gazette Girls
of Grundy County

Horse Trading,
Hot Lead,
and High Heels

Gwen Hamilton Thogmartin
& Ardis Hamilton Anderson

University of Missouri Press
Columbia and London

Copyright © 1994 by
The Curators of the University of Missouri
University of Missouri Press, Columbia, Missouri 65201
Printed and bound in the United States of America
All rights reserved

5   4   3   2   1   98   97   96   95   94

Library of Congress Cataloging-in-Publication Data

Thogmartin, Gwen Hamilton, 1914–
    The Gazette girls of Grundy County : horse trading,
  hot lead, and high heels / Gwen Hamilton Thogmartin
  and Ardis Hamilton Anderson.
        p. cm.
    ISBN 0-8262-0986-6
    1. Thogmartin, Gwen Hamilton, 1914–   . 2. Anderson,
  Ardis Hamilton. 3. Women editors—Missouri—
  Biography. 4. Newspaper editors—Missouri—Biography.
  5. Grundy County gazette (Spickard, MO : 1910)
  I. Anderson, Ardis Hamilton. II. Title.
  PN4874.T416T46   1994
  070.4'1'082—dc20
    [B]   94-28263
                                                        CIP

∞™ This paper meets the requirements of the
American National Standard for Permanence of Paper
for Printed Library Materials, Z39.48, 1984.

Designer: Stephanie Foley
Typesetter: Connell-Zeko Type & Graphics
Printer and binder: Thomson-Shore, Inc.

To the memory of
C. Orville Thogmartin
Kerry Vincent Thogmartin
Dr. Roy H. Anderson
and all the folks we knew at Spickard
a long time ago

Contents

Preface

Then and Now

Gwen

The "then" part of this book does what journalism school and years of writing experience trained us to do—tell the who, what, when, where, why, and how of the years we spent as country editors during the depression days of the 1930s. We were much too young to believe it when people told us women could not buy and operate a country newspaper. Even though journalism school had not really prepared us for the undertaking, and neither of us had any real newspaper experience, we ignored those dire predictions. It never occurred to us we could fail. Perhaps that is why we didn't.

In the 1930s almost every small town, even those with as few as five hundred people, had a newspaper. Now most small town newspapers have disappeared, due in part to the diminishing population of rural areas. Technological advances have created both the ability and the necessity to farm large acreages and have led to the

invasion of corporate farming. Those factors have reduced the population of former trade areas drastically,
and therefore reduced both the available readership and
the need for advertising outlets.

Modern transportation and good roads also have contributed to the demise of the small town newspaper.
Small town merchants can no longer compete with
those in larger cities, with supermarkets, a variety of
clothing stores, automobile and machinery agencies,
fast food chains, and all of the other places offering
life's necessities and luxuries. Often residents of small
towns commute to work in the larger ones. Advertisers,
the lifeblood of the country newspaper, found what advertising they did do brought better results from the
larger newspapers of the county. Because fewer people
spend most of their time in the small towns, there is also
less sense of community than in the 1930s. The social
life has changed drastically, although it has not disappeared in many places. Still, not too many people really
care where their neighbors spent the weekend. Local
items are passé.

In the 1930s, often the only access to information
about current civic and political affairs and entertainment was through the local newspaper. Many homes
could not afford a telephone or radio, and of course
there was no television. At a subscription price of $1.00
per year, the hometown newspaper was about the only
reading matter many folks could afford, and if they
lacked a dollar in cash—as was often the case—they
could always work out a trade with the editor. They enjoyed seeing their names and those of their neighbors in
print. The local news column was sometimes the first
thing read, just to see who visited whom during the
week. As perhaps one reader described it best, "If you

read it in the paper, you can figure it is probably right. Beats gossip."

We discovered, somewhat to our surprise—they didn't tell us this in journalism school either—that a country newspaper could contribute to the sense of pride and unity of a small town. At first the local attitude was "what will those girls do next," but that sense of anticipation kept subscribers coming in with little items or incidents they hoped to see in print. And just as important, it kept subscribers coming in.

Our newspaper was typical of many country newspapers in that it reflects a slice of Americana, a bit of the history of an era in the twentieth-century United States. Its uniqueness is in the fact that we were not only the youngest editors in Missouri but also women who were entrepreneurs on their own.

After we sold the paper, we embarked on other pursuits. Ardis lived in Kansas City and Gwen in Emporia, Kansas, only one hundred miles apart, for more than forty years, and both of us were involved in careers that kept us writing and honing our skills. Writing a book by long distance, sharing material through the mail and making many trips back and forth, proved to be rather impractical and unsatisfactory, however. When Gwen and her son, Clyde Thogmartin, persuaded Ardis she should move to Emporia, the book was only one of the reasons she sold her house in Kansas City, moved to Emporia, and bought a house six blocks from Gwen's. Now, at last, we could do what we had promised each other we would do more than half a century ago. We could write this book.

Acknowledgments

We greatly appreciate the cooperation and skills of the University of Missouri Press staff, especially the director, Beverly Jarrett; our editor, Jane Lago; and the marketing manager, Karen Caplinger. Their ideas and enthusiasm were very helpful.

Without the encouragement of friends and relatives who kept saying, "You ought to write a book," or "You can do it," we might never have done it. This especially is true of Clyde and Janis Thogmartin, Carl and Rita Headrick, and Bill and Dorothy Bowles, and also our friend and attorney, Don Lill, who interpreted contracts and copyrights for only a promise of a copy of the book.

The Gazette Girls
of Grundy County

Chapter 1

Who and Why

Gwen

It seems incredible now, more than half a century later, that two young farm-bred girls should buy a country newspaper during the blackest of the 1930s depression days and should survive to look back upon the experience with loving nostalgia. It seems even more incredible that, when country editors throughout the nation were declaring bankruptcy, those two girls would manage to earn their living, keep ahead of the interest on the mortgage, and still enjoy the experience. But buy the paper we did, my sister, Ardis, and I, and although country journalism wasn't at all like fiction and Hollywood had portrayed it, it was just as exciting—and frankly a lot more work and worry.

In all honesty, we met with very few of the problems we expected to have. Coping with the millions that we never anticipated made our years as editors of the *Grundy*

1

County Gazette a time we have remembered with un-modest pride and satisfaction all our lives. If we accomplished little else, we built our confidence so that we felt we could face anything we might meet in the future.

Ardis had acquired a college degree and fulfilled her lifelong goal of being a high school English teacher. I had managed a couple of years at the University of Kansas School of Journalism before the depression, dust storms, grasshoppers, and the resultant crop failures shrank the family income too short to cover college expenses. Then I had one difficult term in a country schoolroom the size of a cracker box with twenty-two children aged five to sixteen, grades one to eight, all inclusive. I, in case of doubt, was "teacher," although at times I thought I was learning more than the pupils. I received $45.00 per month for my efforts at teaching, janitoring, fire building, trying to avoid long-standing district conflicts, and driving six miles through mud or boarding at an unmodern house that sheltered seven to a dozen people most of the time. Fortunately they were the kind of people who are sometimes described as the salt of the earth, or I would never have survived, but I learned some valuable lessons in relationships that served me well later on in my newspaper experiences.

Ardis was equally weary of the ills of the teaching profession in the 1930s, but success was hers except from the standpoint of her own happiness. Both of us wanted the kind of work at which—win or lose—we could try out our own ideas. And, as we pointed out to each other, we didn't have much to lose. At least I didn't. Ideas came easy and often to me, and didn't cost a thing.

Furthermore, we were haunted by the abiding fear that we were growing old and accomplishing nothing.

Fifteen years later this was amusing. More than a half century later it is hilarious. When we bought the paper, I had not yet been old enough to vote, and Ardis had voted in only one presidential election. That is how young we were.

Ardis and I had both loved to read all of our lives and both enjoyed writing, but in 1935 even top-flight members of the fourth estate* were pounding the pavements for positions or even jobs. Hopes of getting writing work of any kind sank lower with every interview I had.

It was summer vacation, and Ardis and I were sewing cheesecloth curtains and ten-cents-a-yard (top-quality) yellow percale bedspreads for our big attic room, when I said casually, "Let's buy a run-down country newspaper and build it up. We can keep it a year or two and sell it when times get better and buy a larger one. By the time we get old—thirty-five or forty—we'll be set for life. We might even retire and freelance."

Ardis, the precise and practical, carefully fastened off a thread and snipped the needle loose neatly with her

---

*We are surprised now when people ask, "What is the fourth estate?" It is an old term often used earlier in the twentieth century, seldom used now, but still somewhat understood. "There are three estates in Parliament: the Lords Spiritual, the Lords Temporal and the Commons; but in the reporters gallery yonder there sat a fourth estate in the realm, more important than they all." This statement, the basis for the designation of journalists as the "fourth estate," was attributed to Edmund Burke, writer, English statesman, and member of the British Parliament in the late 1700s. It was not in his published works, but Thomas Babington Macaulay, English historian, credited Burke with the statement in "Hallam's Constitutional History," *Edinburgh Review*, September 1828.

scissors. Ardis never bites threads or leaves loose ends even in an absentminded moment.

"What will we use for money to buy the first one?" she inquired.

"Your savings and a mortgage," I grinned at her. "I'm glad you're so thrifty."

"Well, really!" she exclaimed, with a touch of acidity. "Do you have any money at all?"

"Oh, I have enough to live on," I assured her. "If it doesn't cost more than twenty dollars a month and we get the thing to paying a profit in two months."

It sounded pretty wild, even to me, and knowing Ardis's dyed-in-the-wool Republican conservatism, I wonder how she ever figured out what her percentage would be, but the idea really intrigued her. I continued to paint pretty pictures of our future prosperity until she agreed it might be worth looking into.

"With your salesmanship ability and my financial genius," she observed dryly, "I don't see how we can fail."

We grew so enthusiastic that the attitude of our family and friends failed to daunt us. They hinted that any time two girls wanted to buy a country newspaper something must be wrong. We tried to explain that in our case it was boredom with our present occupations, a desire to write, and the necessity of creating our own jobs if we were to do work we liked. Reluctantly, our family agreed to let us look into the situation. At least we assumed the lack of opposition meant they sanctioned the idea.

We did not consider seriously the sacrifices we would have to make to do the thing we wanted to do, but at no time during the tough, fascinating, often worried but never dull days that followed did we have any regrets. It was all a part of the game, and as such we accepted everything that came along.

Ardis

Gwen could always be trusted to come up with something original. The clever designs for the yellow percale bedspreads were her idea, and I have to admit they made an attractive room, although I hated to think about ironing the spreads.

Both of us had wanted to write ever since we started grade school. I got the yen when I was six years old and wrote my first composition about a rabbit we had seen playing in our garden. I don't know when the urge first struck Gwen, but books and reading had been our favorite pastime ever since we learned to read—at the age of four in each case—and English was our best subject in school.

By the time Gwen was halfway through that unhappy time trapped in the cracker-box schoolhouse, I realized she had not been cut out for a teacher, although she loved children and was equally at ease with people of all ages. The odds were against her from the beginning, of course. Not every country school had so many pupils, of all grades, with IQs ranging from superior to moron, all cooped up in a tiny building constructed years ago when the total enrollment was exactly three. By nature she would have preferred to enjoy her students rather than to direct them, but rural school boards held no brief with anything less than good "discipline"—the prime requisite of a "qualified" teacher in the 1930s. It is hard to discipline a pupil who is less than two years younger than the teacher, too.

To make things worse, if they could be, the school was in the district where we both had lived until I was ready for high school, and some people remembered her as the little girl who had won everybody over just by smiling at them. They didn't realize she had grown up in spite of her barefoot height of five feet nine inches, which I greatly envied.

That was the fall following the dry summer of 1934 when the leaves fell in August and the corn shriveled up as though scorched by a prairie fire. When the rains came finally, they were junior floods with no letup.

I didn't see how she could have drawn a worse deal. But, in spite of it all, she wrote clever letters that would put me in stitches as she described the cute doings of her "Dotty," age five, or the latest outrages of the family whose parents sewed their three children into their underclothing in the fall and expected them to stay there until spring. It might be a church party, a chocolate cake she had baked, the duet she had sung, the violin solo she had played, or the stunning new navy corduroy suit she had made for practically nothing, but she never lacked a subject, and she always made the most routine thing sound interesting.

Teaching had been a great disappointment to me. I had planned to make a lifetime career of it with the hope eventually of getting into college teaching and doing some freelance writing on the side. In the early 1930s, however, colleges were letting their younger teachers go instead of taking more on as the depression years found enrollments decreasing and funding for colleges lessening. Eager to become self-supporting and to pay back money borrowed for my last year in college, I was thrilled when I was selected from one hundred and fifty applicants for a position teaching English and Latin in a northern Kansas high school.

I soon learned that there are some things they don't

teach you at the university—such as that high school students do not just automatically love English because their teacher does and that you can gain the animosity of practically the entire school by flunking the best football player in two subjects. It wasn't my fault he skipped school for two weeks, didn't make up his work, and ignored the rule that said players had to pass three out of four courses in order to be on the team. And, as I found out, if the play director didn't cast the most popular members of the class in the junior play regardless of either their acting ability or their disposition to cooperate with you—or lack of same—the director's status plummeted to zero.

The first year was an endurance test, but I was too busy to realize how hard I worked. I paid back a six-hundred-dollar debt and saved enough to return to the University of Kansas during the summer to study toward my master's degree. As soon as the second year's term opened I began putting cash in the bank—half to two-thirds of my salary—and I'll admit I was somewhat cocky about my ability to budget when most of my fellow teachers borrowed money to tide them over the summer vacations.

I followed all the rules I had ever heard about being a good teacher. I played piano for services at the First Presbyterian Church, directed school plays (a responsibility often expected of the English teacher in small high schools), kept reasonably good order in my classrooms by sheer force of determination, and tried to be patient and understanding with the students. I even attended Parent-Teacher Association meetings, but in all honesty that was in self-defense—in that town the meetings were devoted to talking about the teachers who weren't present. Yet I recall somewhat ruefully that I didn't feel I was especially popular or even appreciated.

Our qualifications as editors might not be so bad, I reasoned silently, as Gwen, half in jest, continued to elaborate on her newspaper idea. Gwen had taken several courses in reporting and feature and creative writing. She had originality and a sense of humor. She met people well and would have a zest for the outside work. My journalism experience was limited to a course in copyediting and headline writing, which I had persuaded the head of the journalism department into letting me take for graduate credit one summer, even though I lacked an hour of prerequisites. I was confident, however, of my knowledge of grammar, my ability to understand the structure of a news story, and my solid grounding in English, which would be a help in editing copy and reading proof.

I was to find out that running a country newspaper requires something more than a knowledge of grammar and syntax or even of writing with originality and zest.

Chapter 2

What: Our Paper

Gwen

The first problem was to find a paper we could buy with a down payment of $500.00 and a debt of not more than $1,500.00. That would leave us with a few hundred for operating expenses until we "started making a profit." We knew we wanted a Linotype machine, since setting type by hand, as some country newspapers of that era were still doing, would leave us little time to write, interview, and pursue the more interesting phases of newspaper work. Aside from a Linotype, we were vague as to what machinery we would need. Most of our mechanical experience consisted of running a sewing machine—which either of us did with credible skill—or driving a car, which we also did skillfully enough until something went wrong. Then we just called the nearest mechanic. Besides, cars were simple in those days.

No, we didn't know much about printing machinery, I admitted, fingering Ardis's Phi Beta Kappa key with Pi Lambda Theta and Quill Club pins attached, but we were intelligent. We had the grade point averages to prove it. We could learn. We did. Oh, brother, how we learned!

Some thirty Missouri and Kansas editors answered a classified ad that we placed in a Sunday issue of the *Kansas City Star.* The ad read: "Wanted to buy: small Linotype equipped newspaper. Low down payment; good field for development." The large number of replies should have warned us that editors were none too prosperous, but we intelligent girls never gave that a thought.

We selected the most likely sounding letter and started across eastern Kansas in Nancy, Ardis's 1930 Chevrolet, which we listed as one of our major assets. In northern Missouri, that evening, we stayed at a cabin camp, the forerunner of a motel, and bright and early the next morning we drove the twelve remaining miles to Spickard.

Only it wasn't bright at all, it was just early, when definitely I am never in quite my best spirits. A heavy rain was falling, and our first impression of the town was negative, to put it mildly. It was situated at the edge of what was known as the upper Ozark range, a series of hills that to our Kansas plains vision looked like mountains proper. Every up-and-down street was deeply rutted and running-board deep in mud and water. The paved highway served as the main street, along which most of the business firms were located.

Several burned-out buildings, with their debris of blackened boards and broken bricks, only halfheartedly cleared away, testified to recent fires. The more experienced might have suspected that some of those fires were friction fires caused by the mortgage and insurance papers rubbing together and used the suspicion craftily to bargain with the newspaper owner for a lower price. When we thought of this years later, we comforted ourselves by remembering that this had been our first venture into the world of commerce.

Battered flivvers and bony horses brought bewhiskered farmers clad in faded and patched denim into town. They spat a brown stream of tobacco into the torrent that rushed down the gutters and eyed us with speculative curiosity. Their gaze suggested that frankly they wondered just what business two obviously young girls could have there, and we heard some rather amusing rumors later about their guesses.

It was a rain-drenched, discouraging scene. We came close to turning and running home without ever going near the *Grundy County Gazette.* This was a far cry from the bright little town of our dreams where we were going to show the world how to run a modern, influential newspaper.

But Ardis, who is about five feet two in very high heels and weighed about one hundred four, squared her jaw. "We've come this far," she announced, "so we may just as well go in. Even if we don't like the town or the paper, we might learn something."

"OK," I gulped over the lump of disappointment in my throat, my enthusiasm as droopy from the rain as was the blue tailored cotton dress I had made for this occasion. "Let's go." Never would I admit her nerve could outdistance mine.

We found the paper in a basement with a sidewalk-level entrance on a side street. The street ran downhill across the Rock Island railroad tracks and ended at the Grand River. Up the hill to the east a number of impressive-looking houses of a style known now as Victorian testified to a sometime prosperity.

Carl Castor, the suave editor of the *Grundy County*

Gazette, explained that he wanted to sell the paper because of other business interests. He showed us the books for the four years he had owned the paper. They were satisfyingly if not overwhelmingly in the black. He showed us samples of the additional job work he did—letterheads, envelopes, cards, sale bills, and business forms—with records of the sales. He explained the subscription lists were incomplete because a fire six months earlier had damaged the building in which the paper had been located beyond repair and destroyed all the records. Had we been more experienced, we would have been less impressed with the past six months' business, but I doubt if it would have deterred us from our goal of buying a paper. Even that paper.

He took us for a tour of the shop and introduced us to each piece of machinery. The machinery did not acknowledge the introductions. Most of it just stood mutely and let us try to look intelligent while we felt as foggy as the weather outside.

He assured us that his employee, whom he called Kes, a victim of depression railroad shutdowns, would be available as a printer and Linotype operator. Had we known Cliff Kessler was a highly intelligent former train dispatcher who could earn more in a day when the trains were running than we could pay in a week, we would not have pinned so much faith on that help. In fact, we would not have pinned much faith on any help, but the help problem was new to us then. We had been hired, not hiring, and we had been steeped in such ideas as loyalty, integrity, respect, responsibility, and the notion that an employee was obligated to produce for the employer. In the thirties that was the norm, what got and kept jobs where there were jobs.

Kes turned out to be one of the best employees we

ever had, but with his experience—and his experiences, which I am sure would fill a book of rather lurid reading—I really couldn't blame him for having a cynical attitude at being forced into the position of working for two girls who knew far less about what they were doing than he did. He never let us down, however; he was respectful and always unfailingly helpful with suggestions, and we became good friends, his cynicism about us fading as we progressed.

Castor also introduced us to several other businessmen and women who were friendly and cordial but full of ill-suppressed curiosity. Castor hinted he had other prospective buyers. However, the rain had dampened our spirits and the strain had wearied us to the point that we were unable to make any decision that night. Evening came, and we went back to the cabin camp. We made arrangements to return the next day to give Castor our decision.

We listed the businesses—and potential advertisers—we had observed and those we could glean from the copies of the *Gazette* that Castor had given us: two drugstores, one owned by old-timer D. G. Dennis, and other by newcomer M. I. Brown; two grocery stores, Wilson's and Little's; Pete Taylor's, which seemed to be a sort of department store, selling housedresses and work clothes—overalls and the like—and other merchandise, including groceries; two garages with what Castor had called the best of mechanics; several filling stations; a pool hall; a café; a combined real estate and insurance agency; Schooler's Furniture Store; Young's Lumber Yard; the law office of T. S. Keith; a blacksmith shop; the dental office of Dr. Heck; the offices of two medical doctors, Ewing and McClanaham, and an osteopath, Dr. Nellie Kaiser; a place where the proprietor appeared to be refinishing furniture; and perhaps some we had missed.

We then considerd the businesses in our hometown of Waverly, Kansas, and reflected that the editor there had survived for a number of years on no more than what Spickard appeared to offer. We should have a chance.

The next day the sun played a dirty trick on us. It shown brightly, and the June weather was perfect. The lawns were green and well clipped. Masses of roses, poppies, larkspur, and brilliant hollyhocks popped out magically, encouraged to do their best by the warm, moist air. They sent alluring perfume with every breeze. Washed by yesterday's rain, the town looked clean and bright. Cheered by the fall of moisture, the lifeblood to growing crops, the women appeared on the streets in bright, starched print dresses, and the men laughed and joked with friends. Laborers from the WPA were preparing to surface those streets that had disturbed us yesterday. There was the pleasant hum and bustle of busy, happy people. The whole town, totally unaware of what it was letting itself in for, had put its best foot forward. We bought the paper.

Ardis

In the "good field for development" lay our plans and hopes. We were confident that if we could just make a living and keep up our payments for a few years, we eventually would be able to build up a publication we could be proud of. Then, as Gwen said, we could sell it and buy a larger one in a locality where perhaps we would remain permanently.

I was going to insist on one other thing, I declared as we crossed Kansas City and headed into the Show-Me State on our way to look over the *Grundy County Gazette*. There must be trees. I had spent three years in that little town in northern Kansas where trees were scarce and spindly and refused to turn red-gold in the fall. If Spickard didn't have trees, we would simply turn around and go home. Gwen gave me a look that would have withered the leaves on a tree and remarked dryly, "I hope Spickard has people."

The Missouri countryside was lush and green with plenty of rolling high hills and winding curves. As we drove along Highway 65 toward Chillicothe on the last leg of our journey, we observed that unless the next thirty miles brought an abrupt change there would be trees galore. As for the "good field for development," I was to get that too—and how! In fact the development far exceeded anything either of us had thought possible.

The population of Spickard was approximately six hundred when we moved there in 1935. Hearsay had it that Spickard was named for an early settler, perhaps even a founder, and there were several families with the surname still living there. However, since several of them claimed to be only very distant relatives of the others, we could never verify the story of the name. Grundy County was rumored to have been named for the county in another state from which an early settler came. We never knew for sure.

My first impression of Spickard was that it contained the stickiest, slickest mud I had ever encountered. Most of my driving had been confined to pavement, gravel, or at least a fine top coating of natural sand, characteristic of some parts of Kansas. Kansas mud may be slick or it may be sticky, but it is seldom both at the same time.

This Missouri mud was different; to make it worse, the hills were practically perpendicular. Driving north- ward on Highway 65, we slowed down as we came to the little town of Spickard and looked carefully for a sign announcing the location of the *Grundy County Gazette.* None was to be seen. When we came to the top of the hill that marked the far city limits, we turned back and carefully looked again.

"It must be on a side street," I said, as I guided Nancy off the highway into the slick mud and almost ended up in a tomato patch. We extricated ourselves and found the *Gazette* just off the main street.

At the *Gazette* office, I tried hard to concentrate on figures while the editor, Carl Castor, showed me his books and the job samples. They weren't too clear to me, but according to his explanation we should be able to live and make our payments, especially since he was asking only $25.00 per month, much less than I was accustomed to saving on a salary. Even with a small raise for the printer–Linotype operator, the finances seemed feasible.

The editor told us about the Spickard canning fac- tory, which would open in August. This was a fairly new venture for Spickard and was the result of work by busi- nessmen who had promoted the project in order to help the financial status in their trade territory. It obvi- ously was a source of pride to the community. We took it to be a sign of a progressive community with which we could fit in nicely.

Castor assured us we could depend on printing half the election ballots for the county and on a consider- able amount of job printing, as well as commissions to print legal publications from the county clerk and the probate judge, who were both Republicans. The *Gazette* had always been a Republican paper, and the county usually voted Republican. Twelve of the fourteen lawyers in nearby Trenton were Republicans. He promised to go with us to that county-seat town and introduce us to the county officials and some of the lawyers.

Paid subscribers were fewer than four hundred when we bought the paper, although there were more names on the mailing list. People were as much as five years behind on their subscription payments. Reader interest had lagged, and therefore, we discovered, advertisers were questioning whether advertisements in the local paper were being read. We jumped to the conclusion, perhaps correctly, that Castor was more interested in the job printing and the business end of newspapers than in the journalism side. At any rate, we felt our journalistic efforts were in large part responsible for increasing the circulation to more than twelve hundred during our tenure.

Spickard's majestic elms and brilliant flowers added to my excitement when we returned the next morning and closed the deal. Castor took us to the office of an elderly country lawyer, T. S. Keith, who drew up the necessary papers on an old Oliver typewriter, which he operated quite accurately with two fingers in a hunt-and-peck system. I remembered the rule to read carefully before signing and conscientiously waded through the list of equipment, the seller's promise not to go into a competitive business in Grundy County for at least five years, and the stipulations as to terms.

There was a mortgage to the Peoples State Bank for $400.00 and a second mortgage to the editor for the balance due him after I had made my down payment.

On the second mortgage we were to pay $25.00 the first of each month. This payment included interest on the unpaid balance with the remainder of the payment to be applied each month to the principal.

I insisted Gwen read the contract, too. She seemed to finish in about half the time it took me.

"I hope it doesn't get any colder here in winter than it does in Kansas," I observed while she was reading.

Castor assured me it did not. Come winter I found I had another lesson in store. Fortunately we had the paper underway by then, so it didn't matter whether or not I doubted his knowledge and veracity.

Outside I asked Gwen, "Did you read every word of that contract as I asked you to do?"

"Of course," she assured me. "You said read it. I did. You didn't say I had to understand it." I gave her a sharp look. She was grinning. That was typical in our relationship for the next several years.

Chapter 3

Where: Spickard, Missouri

Gwen

One blistering hot July day two weeks after signing the contracts we followed the truck carrying most of our worldly goods. It was piloted by a couple of Kansas truckers who promptly celebrated their advent from a dry state to a wet state even before reaching Spickard, Missouri.

The truckers were putting the furniture into our rented five-room cottage when we arrived. This house was the only one available for rent in Spickard and cost us $7.00 per month. The furniture we had gleaned mostly from attics of good-natured relatives who may have been happy to get rid of it anyway. I jumped from the car and was nearly paralyzed with horror—the burly truck driver was gleefully tossing a box marked on all sides, "Dishes. Very Fragile." Some of these were family antiques and heirlooms and were irreplaceable. Only my thorough packing saved them. There was a lot of difficulty with our piano, too. They attempted to get it

GRUNDY CO

HOME OF THE SPICKARD CANNING COMPANY

VOLUME 48   ESTABLISHED 1887   SPICKARD, MISS

WE CONTINUE FORMER POLICY

Friendly Co-operation Is Assured To Everyone

We believe it's a grand town to which we, the new editors, have come; everyone we meet is friendly; the neighbors are kind and helpful and the business people cordial and co-operative. It is impossible to express adequately our enjoyment of the spirit with which the Spickard people have welcomed us.

We especially appreciate your kindness in the face of the fact that we know you regret the Caster's leaving--a feeling we can readily understand, for they have helped us wonderfully. We cannot hope to fill exactly their places in the community, but we sincerely wish to make our own place with all of you.

We are proud to be located in such a progressive looking place, for we were much impressed with Spickard's well-kept appearance-- its beautiful homes and trim lawns. In fact we had not been in town four days until no less than five people asked us if we were going to clean up our lawn and we finally became so ashamed of ourselves that we broke over and had the job done.

Our office force--your own Edra Gose and C. R. Kessler-- have proved themselves so helpful and efficient that we've decided we cannot do without them, and we are anticipating with much pleasure the building up of our business with the four of us.

Our paper will continue the high standard set by the recent editor and will carry on its Republican policies. We intend to shoot square ly and sincerely and to co-operate with you for the betterment of the town and the community.

We've met a lot of folks, but there are more of you to meet yet. If we do not see you elsewhere, drop in and get acquainted with us. We hope those of you whom we have already met will come in and let us know you better.

GRAND THEATRE TO

BE REMODELED

The Grand Theatre in Princeton was closed Monday evening to permit remodeling of the building.

A new front and lobby will be built, the balcony removed, a new floor built, and the stage made smaller and moved back several feet. Upholstered chairs will be installed and arranged in three sections with a narrow section on each side and a wide section in the center. A new screen and modern lighting fixtures will be installed. It is expected to require about five weeks of work, and when completed, will make the theatre one of the most modern in this section of the state.

HELEN STEENBERGS

Miss Helen Steen, Mr. and Mrs. L. L. cothe, was married of Stanford, Texas, McMurrp Chapel high noon July 4 was performed by St. Joseph, grand Twenty relatives attended.

Mrs. York is Chillicothe Bu father was fo Grundy Count has many fri wish her well

Mr. York, E. York of dent in the assistant i ment.

Followi was serve uncle an Wimple will ma and w college

PLA

FLOYD MACK GALT A

Floyd Mack, of Gal the Shell filling static mitted suicide Mon taking carbolic acid, Dr. H. C. Kimberlin, made an examination and investigated the morning

Mr. Mack was four tween four and five L. C. Marsh home wh and boards. Mr. Ma into his room to aw breakfast, and foun across the bed with h At first, it was believe the result of a hea services we

THE GRUNDY COUNTY GAZETTE

Published Every Thursday

Ardis H. Hamilton
Editor

Gwendolyn E. Hamilton
Assistant Editor

Subscription $1.00 Per Year in Ad vance

Display Advertising 20 cents pe inch except on contracts

Entered at the Postoffice at Spick ard, Mo., as second Class Mail Rate

MODENA

Hobart Rutherford of near Go- shen was in Modena Thursday.

Nellie Rockey called on Mrs. Ruth Bever Thursday.

Eva Sires had the misfortune of getting her arm broken Tuesday.

Floyd Nigh and Mrs. Rosa Bame took Mrs. Amanda Riley to Prince- ton Saturday to see a doctor.

through the front door, where it stuck. Fortunately another door was unlocked, so they both went to the inside and tried to pull it through. They finally managed to get it in and placed where we told them to put it, apparently unscathed.

If we had not been so tired and furious it would have been funny. We stood by and watched helplessly. "I hope," I seethed, "they try to take liquor back to Kansas and the state patrol catches up with them." "Me, too," Ardis gritted.

Sunday, the next day, we put our house to rights. We carried soft water from the cistern—there was no running water—and warmed it on our kerosene stove, which smoked because we couldn't get it level. We scrubbed every inch of woodwork and flooring. We disinfected closets, swept down the papered walls with a cloth on a broom, cleaned up and arranged furniture, and even hung a few pictures. We worked like fury.

We altered, temporarily with pins, what curtains we had to fit some windows and planned how we could curtain others for a stipend. We made cupboards for dishes out of crates. We were so busy that it was the middle of the afternoon before we became aware of how heavy the traffic was on the street past our house, and remarked it was odd there should be so much traffic on a side street. After the dust continued to roll in as the cars slowed to round "our" corner, it dawned on us we were the attraction. For probably the only time in our lives we were stopping traffic. We were torn between amusement and chagrin, but we realized that clad in shorts and halters at a time when shorts were just coming into fashion in small towns and with bandannas tied around our heads we doubtless had given the good citizens of Spickard an awful impression. They probably regarded us as quite risqué.

To atone for the bad beginning, we pushed most of the unpacked stuff into a back room, hung up our clothes, carried in tubs of water, and scrubbed off the housecleaning dirt. Tired as we were, we dressed to the teeth and strolled down to the post office to mail some postcards home. We counted twenty-two curtains move as we passed, and returned via another street just to prove we didn't mind.

Everybody, it seemed, was curious about "those two girls who bought the *Gazette*." It was weeks later that we found someone had started a rumor that two old maids had purchased the paper. Our obvious youth and the show we managed to put on of sophistication and poise were rather a shock. The good citizens—and maybe even the bad—couldn't help wondering what would become of their paper in the hands of two inexperienced and probably giddy girls. Women in the 1930s just didn't buy newspapers and run them. When a woman asked me what paper our father owned, she looked utterly amazed when I explained he was a farmer.

To us, satisfying the curiosity of the citizens of the Spickard community was just another challenge to be met, as though we needed another one. We decided the best way to do this was to try to show the people we were hard-working, professional, responsible women who had the best interests of the community at heart, and that we could run a newspaper. We still wonder if our inner qualms showed, like a too-long slip beneath a dress hem.

Ardis

The expression I saw on the face of our quiet, matter-of-fact father when he told us good-bye convinced me of the immensity of our undertaking more than any of the warnings we had heard during the two weeks we were preparing to go to Spickard.

Of course Dad had never run a newspaper. Starting out with nothing at the age of fourteen, he had managed to pay off the mortgage on his first farm, marry our mother, purchase for cash a second suburban place where their daughters could be near a high school, give us each music lessons for years, and pay for two years for each of us at the University of Kansas. As far back as we can remember, our parents subscribed to and read the county daily. He loathed owing money, and even during the depression days and Mother's long illness before her death in 1931, he kept square with the world.

Perhaps, I reasoned, as we took turns driving and holding our tiny white kitten, Tarzanna, so called for her propensity for climbing limbs—she could riddle a pair of silk hose in less time than it took to say *Grundy County Gazette*—perhaps Dad thought newspaper work was more hazardous than it really was. Maybe it was the mortgage that concerned him. He couldn't have looked more upset if we had been departing to join the Foreign Legion. It wasn't that he said much—he never did. When I went to college or a teaching job he seemed completely unimpressed, although he always encouraged us to get an education and become financially independent. "An education is something no one can take away from you," he would say. It was little more than two hundred miles to Spickard, but we might have thought he never expected to see us again.

We had made a late start. Tarzanna was restless, and it was hot on the road. Cars then were not air-conditioned. When we reached Spickard at dusk we were in no mood to cope with the slightly inebriated truckers.

Several townspeople just happened around at the moment, and I was embarrassed when one trucker, a man well over six feet tall with corresponding bulk, grabbed me and tried to dance me across the floor. Hastily retrieving what dignity I could, I gave them the check for the amount agreed upon previously and, by coolly ignoring them, gave them no excuse to linger, so they went on their way.

It was then we discovered the electricity had been disconnected when the previous occupants of the house had moved out and that we would be in darkness until Monday. Dragging the springs and mattresses of our twin beds into the southeast bedroom, which seemed be the coolest, we arranged pallets on the floor, slid into pajamas, and eased our aching bodies down as quickly as possible.

The next morning when the sun streamed into our room and awakened us, we had no time to think of aching muscles. Neither of us had ever seen such a dirty house. The piano was in the only wall space it could be placed in, but arranging the rest of the furniture was entirely up to us. Our breakfast set of table and chairs, purchased from a mail-order house to be shipped directly to Spickard, had not arrived. After cleaning as thoroughly as possible, we unrolled the rug and I unpacked my six crates of books and placed them in my bookcase. Kitchen cupboards were scarce, so Gwen salvaged the crates for dishes and kitchen things.

As we worked Tarzanna, a ball of white fur with one tiny gray spot under her chin, romped playfully under our feet. One of a large family of kittens, she had been put out in a pasture to starve when friends of ours rescued her. Now grown fat and healthy on milk from Dad's jersey cow, she was a link from the past and a promise for the future, for we couldn't possibly have pets as long as we were rooming in someone else's home and teaching school. We already felt like householders, as ramshackle as our dwelling was and as much as still remained to be done before it could be really comfortable.

After we had returned from our stroll to the post office to see and be seen, we collaborated on our first article, in which we attempted to tell the readers of the *Gazette* that we expected to carry on and maintain the traditions of the paper, that we would retain the two present employees (one of whom we hadn't even met yet), and that we were eager to get acquainted with everyone and become a part of the community. Gwen did the public relations paragraphs and I the political, a pattern we continued.

Our story completed, we locked the doors—although in a small town doors were frequently left unlocked—and drove to Trenton, a metropolis of some six thousand souls, for dinner and a movie. This also became something of a pattern when relaxation became imperative.

Chapter 4

When: July 1935

Gwen

With an outward show of assurance and with inward quaking, we arrived at our office on Monday morning. Early as we were—it was about 7:30—Kes, the printer-operator, was already there and had the gasoline burner on the Linotype going to heat the metal preparatory to setting type. That gasoline burner was to cause us many nights' work during the next few years. Unless it was handled by an expert, it often became temperamental on us and refused to heat.

Cold metal would not cast the slugs—the lines of type—and metal that became too hot, when the burner refused to burn low, caused "squirts," pieces of metal hotter than 500 degrees that would squirt from the machine and make a tedious cleaning job necessary. If we were lucky the metal failed to hit the operator. When it did, a small but thorough burn resulted. All of our operators and we ourselves when we learned to use the Linotype became adept at springing from our chairs in

FOURTH GENERATION IN SCHOOLER'S CHAIRS

The fourth generation of the W. B. Wyatt family will rock in chairs purchased from C. E. Schooler's furniture store.

Mrs. Earl Robbins bought a child's rocker for a Christmas gift to her grandniece, Sandra Sue Pickett, at Schooler's this week. Sandra Sue is a daughter of Mr. and Mrs. Ronald Pickett of Princeton and a greatgrandchild of Mr. and Mrs. W. B. Wyatt. They, their children, and their grandchildren have had rockers from the Schooler store

FREE TICKETS GIVEN!

In cooperation with the Fontinelle stock company which plays in the Schooler building here each Thursday evening, the Gazette plans to offer four free tickets to these plays each week.

Persons who have paid their subscriptions during the past week will be eligible to receive these tickets and their names will appear in the classified column of the Gazette. Read the classifieds regularly — and go and enjoy these plays if your name is listed.

SMITH OR SMYTHE?

They're both nice, so we won't tell their names or how we learned it, but it's our year's best campaign story.

"I'll certainly appreciate your support," a candidate concluded "electioneering" a lady. "By the way, what is your name? I should know."

She hesitated, wanting badly to say "Jones," but she finally admitted it.

She was his opponent's mother.

OTHERWISE FRIENDS

Eight-year-old Johnnie Poe Vaughn, an ardent young Democrat, who recently visited his aunt, Mrs. Maude Dean, Franklin township Republican committee woman, formed quite a friendship with Mrs. Fred Shannon over their mutual interest in the Shannon's attractive little black and white pup.

Being assured that Mrs. Shannon was a Democrat, Johnnie Poe became quite confidential. "I'm a Democrat, too," he asserted. "The only trouble I ever have with these folks down here is over politics!"

AIN'T NO FAVOR

Herbert Brown, who won the Republican nomination for prosecuting attorney, told it on himself.

As it was his first time to run and, naturally, his first to win, he was as excited as a schoolboy at a football game. When the results came in Tuesday night, East Marion reported 12 for him and 12 for his opponent.

"What was that?" he askked of Bob Packwood, Republican Times editor.

"Twelve _ Twelve," Bob replied.

"In whose favor?" Brown heard himself saying.

TO YOU: NOT FAR

L. O. Bandy contributes one:

Mr. Bandy and Kenneth Persell made a trip to Arkansas recently, and as they were traveling along some of the Ozark hills they overtook one of the local residents and asked him to ride. The individual declined with thanks. "I'm just going a couple of looks down the road," he explained.

the opposite direction from where we knew the squirt would spew out. A slight hiss indicated a forthcoming squirt. Visitors sometimes jumped nervously when a sudden clatter indicated someone had knocked his or her chair over to escape the squirt. We grew so accustomed to the sound we didn't even turn unless someone asked for the burn salve. Most men operators sported bits of linotype metal on their trouser legs, and we girls learned to keep a heavy denim printer's apron over our laps.

Edra, a former beauty operator who had become a reporter for Castor because even beauty operators were out of jobs, also had arrived. In all honesty, the first issue was mainly the result of Kes's and Edra's familiarity with the work. However, I wrote a few features, we both met businesspeople, and we instigated a few of our own ideas as well as some of Kes's suggestions about front-page makeup. The changes were enough to establish us as the owners and to bring compliments from appreciative subscribers. The praise went to our heads to the extent that we never hesitated to try out any ideas we had from then on. Usually the innovations brought favorable comment, which proved nothing except that most people have a bit of spirit of adventure and enjoy a change of routine sometimes. We have always thought that being young and being women was to our advantage in this situation. People acted as though they really wanted us to succeed, even the men. We knew quite soon, however, that had we been married, especially with children, the men would have thought the male member of the family should be "boss."

As far as we know, ours was the first country newspaper to eliminate the column rule, the thin line between columns of news. When we decided to make the change we wrote quite an article about the modern typefaces we had added and intimated that dropping the column rule was another modern technique. It had been done before, but we wonder if the first instigator was motivated by the same reason we were. We honestly and sincerely thought the paper was easier to read and more attractive without the rule, but we might not have had the courage to make such a departure from the orthodox in printing had it not been that our rule simply wore out and we couldn't afford to replace it. It was so worn that it insisted on working up on the press and cutting through the paper unless we made frequent stops to pound it down. Many papers afterward adopted the same style, but we modestly took credit for being one of the first.

Our first day at the office was a wearing one, and in the melee of meeting dozens of people who seemed to find some strange excuses for coming in, we scarcely noticed a slender young man named Orville who contributed a gratis column just because he liked to write. In fact he was in once or twice a week for a year before we discovered he and I were within six weeks of the same age. He would borrow a book, read the exchanges— the country weeklies and dailies from that part of the state—talk, and tell us of his latest success in selling a story or a poem. He owned a little handpress, too, and boned up continually on printing by reading our trade magazines. Pretty soon he was telling us things about printing in a quiet, unobtrusive way, and within a year or so he was having quite an influence on the typography of the *Grundy County Gazette*.

From the start our newspaper definitely had our stamp on it. To others it probably looked like any ordinary country newspaper, but to us it was superior, like one's own children. As we learned and grew and improved, the paper improved, too, and the proudest moments of our lives were when we received prizes in press association contests a couple of years later. Recognition from your peers is always satisfying. Then we knew our desire to find expression in the creation of a newspaper was not an idle longing. Some of our dreams had materialized.

We reserved the front page for news stories. Church notes, classified ads, and "locals," those small items people loved to read about visits, trips, and daily life events, we gave special places on pages 2 and 3. A death would be reported on page 1, but the obituaries were on an inside page. We chose an outline type for the front-page name of the paper, because we felt the sheet had been overpowered by the heavy bold type that had been used there. We tried to balance headlines, make them suitable to the length or importance of the story, and just in general make a good-looking paper. We made the changes as fast as we could afford to, and most of them were completed by 1938. Members of the community responded favorably, watched for changes, and seemed to have the idea they were involved. In fact, they were. Their interest and pride in their paper encouraged us to keep trying new things.

Ardis

On that first day at the office, as people swarmed in, I felt more confused by the hour with trying to say the right thing, remember names, round up the electric-power man to connect our house lights, and a dozen other chores that popped up. I became initiated, too, into that little thing called operating expenses in short order, for in spite of the fact that our equipment included a four-ton press, which we named Old Bertha for no particular reason, and a top-heavy Linotype, neither of which could have been moved away without everyone in Spickard knowing it, we were expected to pay rent in advance and make utility deposits.

Kes was setting type. The Linotype (printers, we found, usually referred to it as the "machine") was clicking rhythmically at the touch of his capable fingers, its long arm picking up the used letters, called mats, and distributing them back to their magazine for redistribution with almost human precision. This fascinated me, even more so when I learned that our Linotype was a Model K and was supposed to be a rebuilt Model One; if this was true, it meant it had been built before the turn of the century. Of course that wasn't so long ago in 1935.

Occasionally Kes would get up for one reason or another; this was always a mistake, since there were only two chairs in the room, and with the large number of visitors someone was certain to sit in his chair. He would quietly watch for his chance to retrieve it and return to work. Finally, I went up to Schooler's Furniture Store and bought three used straight-back chairs for a dollar each—our first addition to the office equipment.

We had little else except a long table that served many purposes and an old typewriter on which Edra pounded out her locals, so I started inquiring around and was fortunate a few days later to find an oak rolltop desk owned by Mrs. T. S. Wilson, who lived in one of the beautiful houses on the hill. Instead of paying for it out of the fund placed in the bank for the *Gazette* until we could realize a profit, or at least collect for the ads and job printing, I wrote a check on my personal account, a trick I often resorted to to keep a respectable balance in the newspaper account. We had brought two typewriters with us, a standard and a portable that needed repairs. With a newly acquired bargaining ability born of desperation, I traded the portable plus a small cash difference for a good standard for Gwen.

Toward the middle of our first afternoon we noticed among the stream of callers a very large man with a receding hairline, a high squeaky voice, and a huge, ugly bulldog. Fred McGuire, editor of the *Grundy County Missourian,* the Democratic weekly at Trenton, owner of the voice and the dog, was our most formidable competitor. A former resident of Spickard, McGuire had many friends there, and he lost no chance to filch all the Spickard business he could obtain, especially in the job printing department.

We probably were not very forgiving about the fact that he never hesitated to take business away from us, even though he, unawares, was responsible for the moniker we enjoyed. Looking us over with ill-concealed amusement and derision for our choice of a newspaper and observing my minute stature, Gwen's obvious youth, and our equally obvious (to a member of the profession) lack of experience, he inquired with a sort of gloating leer, "Do you babes of the fourth estate think you can really run a newspaper?"

"Of course," Gwen assured him coolly. You'd never know it if she had ever had a doubt. But the name, *Babes of the Fourth Estate,* was overheard and stuck. Our fun came when eventually it became a term of affectionate respect. Later in the summer McGuire was to tangle with my young sister in a way that, to my intense satisfaction, taught him not to play in her yard of swift answers again.

Presently Castor paid us a call and went with me to

Trenton to meet officials at the courthouse while Gwen
kept shop at the *Gazette*. Chubby George Mapes, with
sparkling blue eyes and a yellow fringe of hair around
his baldness, welcomed me with the friendliness that
made him the high vote getter in every election and so
popular that Democrats didn't even run a candidate
against him for county clerk. His deputy was Mary McRae,
a slender young woman with dark graying hair and the
entire business of the county at the tips of her quiet,
capable fingers. She became one of my best friends.

Probate Judge D. F. "Doc" Warren was equally pleasant, invited us to come in whenever we were in Trenton,
and promised to continue to send the legal notices for
our part of the county to be published in the *Gazette*.
Publication of those notices was one of most lucrative
sources of revenue, and we were proud that the *Gazette*,
with its record of continuous publication, qualified as a
legal newspaper. We were careful never to lose that status by missing an issue, but it was not always easy.

Then we stopped at the office of the *Republican-Times*
and I was introduced to the publisher, Mrs. Carrie Rogers
Clark, who at age seventy still kept a firm hand on the
county's daily, founded some sixty years before by her
father, the late Colonel W. B. Rogers. I also met the
business manager, Ray Van Meter, whom she had reared
and educated as her adopted son; and Bob Packwood,
the young University of Missouri School of Journalism
graduate who was editor. They, too, were friendly, and
their cordial invitation to call on them if we ever
needed help gave me an inner glow that rekindled my
determination to make the *Gazette* worthy of such splen-
did encouragement. Babes we might be, but we could
grow up in the fourth estate.

We needed that glow to warm our spirits many times

during the ensuing months of growing pains. Small newspapers pay their employees weekly but collect their accounts monthly, if they are lucky. We had had a number
of miscellaneous expenses that had sent our bank balance skidding rapidly, but promptly on the first of the
month we deposited our $25.00 payment to Castor as
per arrangement. After a number of months, when this
had become standard procedure, we noticed a sort of
pleased surprise at the bank that we were keeping up
our end of the agreement. We heard later that Castor
had bragged around town that he would be back inside
three months with both the *Gazette* and our down payment. Had we ever entertained any thoughts of quitting, that boast would have burned them up in us. We
would probably have stopped eating to make those payments if necessary. Babes indeed! The ghosts of our
pioneer Kansas ancestors whose roots were in Scotland
stood behind us.

School had not yet opened when we made one of
the first changes—we dropped the "ready-print," which
formed four pages of our eight-page paper. Sometimes
called "patent insides," the ready-print consisted of syndi-
cated articles, recipes, and features, printed on one side
of a sheet of newsprint and sent us each week by Western
Newspaper Union. We printed local news on the blank
side of the sheet. Many small newspapers had followed
the practice of using ready-print, but we had bought
the *Gazette* mainly to gain experience in writing, and it
seemed foolish to spend money for material we thought
would be less interesting to our readers than local news.

Gwen had discovered that there were a number of
Civil War veterans living in the vicinity and planned a
series of features based on their reminiscences. We decided to go to six pages printed in our own office and

emphasize the local angle. Edra thought we were committing suicide, but Kes was cooperative, even though it meant more typesetting for him. We helped as much as possible by typing the handwritten country correspondence—that is, the news from various rural communities—to give him legible copy, by putting in the "corrections"—replacing the lines in which we found typographical errors with corrected lines in the Linotype galley forms after we had proofread the type—and by doing other chores around the shop. We learned to hand set advertising or special headlines that the Linotype couldn't handle.

"Why didn't you do it before?" and "We always wondered why a newspaper used that stuff in the first place; I never read it" were typical of the comments when our first paper came out sans ready-print. The Civil War stories were warmly received. There was a wealth of material, and we kept finding more as our subscribers would read of one veteran and tell us of a relative who might have another. People loved being involved in the paper. We felt as though we were making a worthwhile contribution to the history of the community, and as it turned out all but two of the veterans she interviewed were gone to their reward within the next eighteen months.

In addition to her longer features, Gwen was always on the lookout for short, human-interest items—an outstandingly beautiful garden of flowers, a clever remark by a child, an unusually intelligent animal, or an amusing incident. These she wrote up to fit into two or three inches of type, and Kes figured out a way to set them with stars all the way around to create a boxed effect. We called them boxed features, and soon the town was using the term too.

People would call on the phone and say, "I have a boxed feature for you." They felt it was an honor to furnish us with a boxed feature, and our thrill—and their thrill—knew no bounds the first time one was reprinted in the "Missouri Notes" of the *Kansas City Times,* a column gleaned from pertinent or witty comments from the state's publications. Gwen had the most boxed features because she did more outside work, but we both had our share, and finally it became so much a regular thing to see one reprinted each week that if we didn't make "Missouri Notes" we were disappointed. Spickard loved getting in "Missouri Notes," and we would be just as pleased with the first as with the last of up to a dozen people who would call us to tell us we had made "Missouri Notes" again.

Before we discontinued our ready-print, however, it was a means of our getting out of a very tight spot that was all my fault. When we bought the *Gazette* a bond issue had just been approved for funds with which to pave Spickard's streets. There had been an error in the publication of the notice of the election, though, and it was necessary to set a date for another election to be held after the notice could be republished correctly for four consecutive issues.

At that time we were printing the paper on Wednesday nights and mailing it to go out on the rural routes Thursday morning. On this particular Thursday morning I discovered almost immediately what I had been too tired to notice the night before—the notice of the bond election, which was to run for the final time, had been left out.

I just went home and went to bed. I couldn't face Kes and Edra when the town found out that it would remain in the mud forever and ever. I was too exhausted from spending long hours at the shop and helping with the laundry, cleaning, and housework late at night over the protest of my soft schoolteacher muscles. We didn't do a lot on Thursdays in the shop, so I knew I wouldn't be especially needed. Gwen was there.

By afternoon I felt slightly better and decided to go on living. I arose, straightened up the house, and had just had a bath, combed my hair, and put on fresh makeup when Gwen came home.

"Everything is all right," she said. "Go on breathing. We had just been sitting around all day. Kes kept saying he guessed he'd tear up the forms,* but he hadn't done it yet when Mayor Ashbrook came in and said for us to run a few extra copies of the notice and he'd tell us whom to send them to. So I hunted around and found a few pages of ready-print we hadn't used and Kes took some other stuff out of the local page, inserted the legal, and we ran the front and back pages on the back of the ready-print. Edra took them to the post office and said they were some copies that had been left out of the mailbag."

The bonds carried, and to this day so far as we know

---

*Tearing up the page forms referred to the weekly job of taking out all the things that would not run again—the Linotype metal slugs of news stories, all spacing material, and the hand-set type that had to be redistributed in the proper type cases. It was a job that once done could not be undone without as many hours of work as it had taken to lay out the forms in the first place. Only "standing" ads (those that would run again) and "ad signatures" would remain. Ad signatures were the names of the advertisers who would change copy but leave their names in the same type—an identification as easily recognized as the names themselves.

only a handful of people were ever aware that the rock streets Spickard practically wore out during the next fifteen or so years weren't strictly legal.

After that, I instigated a system of preparing a list of all ads and legals to be published each week, and we checked the page proofs or the forms to be sure none had been omitted.

Chapter 5

My Sister, Ardis

Gwen

Looking back, neither Ardis nor I will take too much individual credit for the success of our venture. Without her, I realize I might never have swung it. Without me, she might have, but I know she feels I made some contributions. I like to think I did, anyway.

When we first went to Spickard, several curious subscribers asked, "Are you girls really sisters?" People in Grundy County were divided into three groups as far as we were concerned—subscribers, advertisers, and all the rest who might become one or the other. We assured them we were.

One asked, "Full sisters?"

We assured her again, but she always looked at us dubiously. In some ways we looked and acted so differently, our personalities were so opposite, that it was hard for people to believe we were even related. But on the few occasions we allowed anyone to witness a sisterly tiff—we saved our real fights for private hear-ings with only each other present—they were usually convinced.

My five feet nine inches, rather casual manner, and calm bearing were such a contrast to Ardis's five feet two of pure, unadulterated, though dignified, spunk. Ardis always looked, acted, and even walked with a firm setting of her size-five shoe as though she knew exactly where she was going and why, and she expected everyone else to be as well organized and unswerving. For several hours she would plow methodically through all of the work that had accumulated on her desk, carefully disposing of or filing each thing as she came to it, and when she had finished declare, "Now my desk is clean. Maybe I can get something done." She never did understand why Kes and I would laugh—we never could convince her she had already gotten something done.

My method was to sort everything over hastily, scrap whatever could be scrapped, stack the rest for future reference in order of importance (and scrap some of that eventually if possible), and get right at the business that I determined to have the highest priority, or to be the most interesting. When the two coincided, as in researching or interviewing for or writing a story, that was nice. We have never figured out which method accomplished the most, but we still tend to work that way. She likes detail. I go for the broad picture.

The only physical characteristics we have that are alike are high cheekbones and a tendency to put on weight where anyone standing behind us could notice it. Fortunately we lived on a budget, had little time to cook rich food, and were so active that the latter was no problem when we had the *Gazette*.

Ardis's hazel eyes, nearsighted behind the glasses she wore, were always serious. She always maintained she had no sense of humor and never dared go to church on Sunday morning if someone had told her a joke on Saturday night. She might get the point and laugh. I used to beg her to relax and live a little. One time everything had coasted along nicely for a week or so, the payroll was in the bank, and there was even a little left over for once. She heaved a big sigh and looked pensively off into space.

"What in the world is the matter now?" I inquired exasperatedly.

"I just wonder if I'm forgetting something," she said seriously. "I can't think of a single thing to worry about." She looked quite perplexed at my burst of laughter.

Her capacity for work, however, was unexcelled. After I was dead on my feet, she was still able to keep her eyes open and set type or make up the paper. At times the glamour had all worn off for me and it was only pride and a dogged determination not to let her outdo me, and a strong sense of fairness that wouldn't let me shirk, that kept me plugging. Her affection for the *Gazette* went deeper than that. It was her life.

Ardis had always been a person to whom possessions meant a lot—not for monetary value, which to her was only a minor mark of success, but as something she had created, that was really hers. She seldom quite trusts people; she never trusts emotions. Unless people can share with her the kind of conversation that appeals to her really fine intellect, she seldom carries on much of a conversation with them. She doesn't always speak the tongue of the masses—especially the masses of a small Missouri hill town at that time. She has little small talk.

But she had plenty of fight in her, and no sacrifice was too great for her to make for the sake of the paper. She never sought personal glory. When I ran out of enough time to do both the Trenton and Spickard ad beats with all the reporting and feature writing, she took the Trenton one, even though she had to steel herself to do it and selling scared her to death. Soon, however, she began to enjoy stimulating contacts with the business and professional people of the larger community, and eventually she built up a successful clientele there.

Ardis had a sense of honor and an honesty I have never seen excelled. If she owed a bill, it was a duty to pay it promptly. She felt shamed and degraded if it wasn't and a pride when it was. She just assumed everyone else felt as she did and was always surprised when other people failed to take care of their debts in the same way. Only when people were afflicted with bad luck beyond their control or with ill health did she relax in this opinion, and her attitude made her a pretty good collector in spite of the fact she didn't think she was.

Ardis was never unkind or threatening; there was just something in her manner that brooked no stalling. My tendency was to feel sympathy for the unfortunate in spite of the fact that I always thought I was more in the business for the money than she was. I might let collections coast if people were hard-pressed (and in 1935–1938 who wasn't), especially if they had small children.

Ardis had no sympathy for the WPA worker who liquefied his meager check at the nearest bar or liquor store before his large family had the barest of the necessities of life, and when he was seriously injured in an automobile accident as the result of his drinking, she refused to give to the fund some of the citizens made up to aid him in getting an artificial leg on the theory he was hardly worth helping now and would probably do no better. However, I caught her giving his wife some clothes she could still have worn or remodeled, because she knew the woman could wear them or use them for some of the oldest girls.

Ardis had—and has—a terrible inferiority complex about her looks. She was positive she was hopelessly plain, so she made an extra effort to be flawlessly groomed, even around home. I never knew her in those days before wrinkle-free fabrics to wear a dress twice without pressing it or a pair of hose twice without washing it. Without running water and thermostat-controlled electric irons, that was not convenient. She was a bit vain about her petite figure, even though she hated being short. We both sewed and enjoyed making our dresses, which was lucky economically.

As a matter of fact she wasn't homely at all. She had a beautiful high forehead with a widow's peak, a fashion plus at that time, but she failed to enhance that forehead by lining it almost always with a worried frown. Her sudden wide smile was charming. She disgustedly called her eyes "dishwater green," but they were more expressive than she knew when lighted with interest. Her hands were small and smooth, nicely shaped, but she would not hesitate to sacrifice them to do inky newspaper chores. The instant she was through, however, hand lotion and nail polish went back on.

It was never easy for Ardis to make casual or many close friends or for her to enter into social events with people who were only acquaintances, but at a political or a town meeting where the issues seemed vital she could forget herself, and she never failed to make a good point in a planned or impromptu talk. Thus stimulated she would impress the dignitaries and powers-that-be without thinking about it. I always tried to convince her it was easier to flash a grin, joke a bit, and listen to their opinions with an air of agreeing, but she kept right on doing things the hard way and earned increased respect for herself and the paper steadily.

We remember with pride that our editorials, together with news and feature stories, influenced Spickard voters to back the provision of more adequate and badly needed fire protection, and that "all" our candidates were elected in Grundy County in 1936. Ardis slaved methodically and carefully over well thought out editorials that appealed to whatever intelligentsia read our paper. I dashed off features designed to be read by everybody. What chance did the unsuspecting public have—especially since mere curiosity and a shortage of other reading material probably stimulated their thorough reading of the *Gazette*. Perhaps the real reason we could make a little impact was that we were sincere in our role as hometown boosters.

Ardis's juggling of funds to make them cover necessary bills equaled nothing I have ever seen or heard tell of on this earth, and there were times when I swore she had inherited all the Scottish blood in the family, so thrifty did she become. I secretly admired her for the way she managed and kept the paper on the black side of the ledger.

Her rigid code of ethics (she didn't believe in dating anyone with whom she was associated in business in any way) and her inability to enjoy anyone and everyone almost eliminated all possibilities of dating for her except at occasional press conventions or political rallies in Kansas City or some other place. She just wasn't interested and would far rather spend an evening going over office work or writing an editorial she felt important than go to a movie with someone who might bore her and whom she was certain she would bore. She would be compelled to make an effort at small talk. If she was lonely at times, she preferred that to boredom. She was by nature a lone wolf, and that characteristic in conflict with my gregarious nature did at times cause friction.

She could never quite see just why I preferred taking my fun where I could find it to spending an evening working on a story that might get reprinted in a larger paper, possibly even the *Kansas City Star.* She never quite understood that I found my features in unexpected places when I was least looking for them or that my enjoyment of an evening stimulated my writing and thinking. I wrote for the joy of writing, and for the enjoyment people found in reading what I had written. I was a people person.

Ardis was a career girl from the beginning of her life in country school. Never in the scheme of things did she consider it a possibility that she would give up the independence a career afforded her for a husband and family. She knew she wasn't good at dividing herself and her ambitions, and she had worked too hard to get her education not to make the most of it. If the path she chose at that time seemed selfish to others, it was because they failed to take into consideration that her enormous ambition drove her to seek larger fields where she could serve public interests instead of keeping a home, for which she recognized, with characteristic candor, she had few attributes. Sometime, maybe, but not until she had proved herself to herself.

She realized the much-talked-of rottenness of politics existed, but she believed that sincere, honest people had an obligation to improve those situations, and she worked untiringly toward that end. She took it as a personal failure when the party and issues she supported lost and would be in the depths of gloom for days after an election failed to go her way. As a matter of fact, until 1952 no election had suited her since before 1932. That's a lot of postelection blues, but only in recent years have her convictions wavered. She remarks that her party left her, not she the party. She still registers as a Republican, but she splits her ticket when she despairs of her party leaders.

Ardis's satisfactions during the *Gazette* period came from the intellectual rather than the emotional. In any field of endeavor she has tried, she has not known failure, but she will not be satisfied with herself, for she is always sure she has failed to develop her potentialities. She is confident of her working ability, modest about her talents.

A charter member of the Missouri Press Women, organized in 1937, she was elected a district vice president. When our paper won awards for outstanding news, editorials, and feature stories in statewide contests, I knew it was one of the biggest thrills she would ever have, and I, to whom every day of living usually had some degree of thrill, was pleased it meant so much to her. I made it policy to keep the shop going while she attended press meetings, the only vacations she ever took. Her contacts with that group were a source of enjoyment and pleasure, and she kept her membership as long as she lived in Missouri, which was many years.

Ardis was always tense, always working, always putting the paper first. I was impatient with her sometimes because she allowed herself so little leisure. Once we were invited to a wedding of an elderly widower and a widow. I was friends with the man's daughter, who had invited me, and left the office at noon for the ceremony and luncheon, although it was press day and we were behind schedule. Ardis was furious with me and kept working right on through the lunch hour without eating.

"Just because a silly old man gets married is no reason to make the paper late," she fumed.

"Just because we own a small town paper is no reason to forget to be human," I retorted hotly. There really was no valid reason to think the paper would be even ten minutes later because I attended the wedding. I knew I had my work for the issue in good shape, and I felt that if a good friend who had been kind to us in many ways would be hurt, that was sufficient reason to delay the paper a few minutes if that was the way it turned out.

Who was right? Neither, I suppose, or perhaps both. The point is that the differences in us were good for the paper even if they were sometimes hard on us. The paper was community service for each of us in a different way. Ardis focused on issues; I focused on people. We were unaware we were reaching for the same goals most of the time in different ways. In spite of clashes and occasional heated arguments, occasional hurts and misunderstandings, we came eventually to a greater appreciation of each other and of other people through our associations in business in a way we never would have done otherwise. Our mutual respect and admiration for each other have deepened our affection in the years that have passed since those exciting days when we shared the problems of the *Grundy County Gazette.*

We had fun together at that oftentimes. Owning the paper was fun. Being those "editor girls" flattered our egos. Decorating on a shoestring budget the little houses we rented interested us. Even if our method of balancing the books—working until midnight in our pajamas in the middle of the living room rug with our favorite snack, a dish of ripe olives, between us and invoices stacked around us—might not have been CPA recommended or approved, we liked it that way and felt between us the warmth of friends in addition to that of sisters. At those times we were very close and squabbles faded into lasting insignificance. We were loyal to each other and presented a united front to our little world.

Chapter 6

My Sister, Gwen

Ardis

The qualities that caused the *Gazette* to catch on with its readers almost as soon as we took it over can be credited solely to Gwen. While they appreciated the improvements in accuracy, for which I was in part responsible, they were delighted with the increased news coverage and the addition of features about the people they knew.

Gwen's enthusiasm was boundless, her curiosity irrepressible. Eager to meet everyone in Spickard, she soon knew almost as many people as Edra did. She found stories in things that had been going on unnoticed for years, and when some of these appeared on the front page in major articles, it helped to offset any opposition that could have developed from our firm policy of confining social and personal items, dignified by their own special columns, to other parts of the paper.

Questions came easily to her because of her genuine interest in people. They may have been surprised that she appeared to be as young as they'd been hearing she was, but they practically broke their necks to bring her up-to-date on the history in which the locality abounded and to introduce her to anyone who might have anything to relate.

While she used to say she would willingly give me a few inches of her five-foot-nine height, were it possible, Gwen was too much absorbed in other people to be self-conscious about the fact that she towered over some of the men. She never made the mistake of some tall girls who tried to minimize their height. Once when we were rushing through the Union Station in Kansas City, where we had come to buy Linotype parts, on our way to catch the train back to Spickard, a woman's voice came clearly to us with the remark, "Doesn't that tall girl in the white hat have a wonderful carriage?"

We looked all around, and Gwen was the only person there with a white hat, a simple felt she wore with a black linen suit she had made herself. She was still searching for the girl in the white hat when she saw me laughing. "Thanks, Dad," she murmured. Our six-foot father had always grabbed her shoulders if he caught her slumping and said, "Be proud you are tall."

Gwen had a fresh, clear complexion, even features that seemed to have changed little since she was about three, a friendly grin that went up slightly on one corner and extended to her blue eyes, and slender, supple hands that were especially attractive when she was playing her violin.

Some sisters wear each other's clothing for variety, but the only thing we could trade was our size-six gloves. Her favorite color was blue, but she wore black and white equally well. While I depended on the warm tones of brown, purple, yellow, or rose to keep me in a pleasant frame of mind, she found cool shades complimentary to the calm but warm poise that was hers.

Gwen was so eager to be at the center of things that it was natural that the most interesting stories, especially during the first few months, would be hers. Her regular beat took her out of the office, while copyediting, proof-reading, and seeing that there was enough cash in the bank to cover the checks we had to write kept me chained to my desk. When a good lead did come in, she always wanted to follow it, and there was no question in my mind that her lighter touch, her less formal style, and the bright sparkle of her personality would make it a better story than I could produce.

Gwen sought new situations, adapted herself to them quickly, enjoyed them thoroughly. My adjustments were slow and painful. She accepted an invitation of an acquaintance to attend a "revival" meeting in a little country church of one of the less popular and less affluent denominations. She spent an entire afternoon at a social club formed by a group of farm women, although she could have covered the story just as well with a five-minute phone call. Sometimes it seemed to me she wasted her time chatting with people much longer than could be justified by the one or two apparently unimportant items they gave her, but the result was friends for the paper and a developing goodwill that paid off in the long run with renewed subscriptions, new subscribers, and tips for feature stories as one person told another of the young editors and the way the *Gazette* was perking up.

Whether we were at home or at the office, it seemed as though it was a little easier for her to do things than for me. While neither of us found any difficulty in handling an ordinary news article, I would write, rewrite, and correct the kind of story requiring an original approach. She would come in, dash off a feature in no time at all, and be off again on another venture. True, her spelling was atrocious, her typing average, and there might be a loosely constructed sentence here or there, but the thing was always good.

"What would you do if I didn't use the dictionary for you?" I would ask.

Neither of us was a good speller. It was too much trouble for Gwen, took too much time when there were more interesting things to do, while I was too lacking in visual imagery, probably because until I finally put my pride in my pocket and consented to wear glasses, I hadn't known how much I had been missing and hadn't formed the habit of noticing things.

Gwen would grin at my exasperation and give me a flip reply. "Oh, I can count on you. You always will. Ardis the accurate," she would tease. Sometimes I wondered what would happen if I really did refuse to go over her spelling, but I never quite dared to put it to the test. Of course as long as Kes was there, it wouldn't gave mattered. He was an excellent speller. In fact he caught errors I missed, to his great satisfaction and ill-hidden glee.

One day after we had had the paper only a few weeks, Gwen came in looking radiant and displayed a pair of beautiful walnut bud vases with long, slender stems. She had discovered that a number of Spickard men pursued a woodworking hobby, and she had been interviewing them. One of them was Jimmy Brokaw, an energetic little man who was a wizard with electricity and clever with almost anything he could invent or make with his hands. He had a sharp mind and extremely definite convictions. Like many capable people in 1935, he was out of steady employment; when not occupied with occasional repair jobs at home or in Trenton, he spent his time with a handmade lathe on which he turned exquisite pieces that he gave to his family and friends. When Gwen admired the bud vases, he promptly gave them to her.

Typically generous, Mr. Brokaw came to call on us the following Sunday afternoon and brought another sample of his art, a set of huge wooden buttons carved from honey locust.

"Do you like these?" he asked me.

"They're beautiful," I exclaimed, marveling at the way he had displayed the grain of the wood and the smoothness of the finish.

"I made these for my daughter-in-law," he confided, "but if you like them I'm going to make some for you. I gave your sister the bud vases and I want you to have something too."

He was as good as his word. I have worn out half a dozen coats and suits trimmed with the enormous buttons that I still treasure, and wherever I have been they have never failed to evoke comment. The light wood of the honey locust was especially suited to my favorite browns and golds, and I still thrill at the memory of his thoughtfulness. But it was Gwen's interest that brought me the buttons.

Gwen's feature on the local woodworkers—their output ranged from cigarette boxes to desks to tables—received considerable attention. Awakened to a new appreciation of ordinary things in its daily routine, Spickard found other material for her, and seldom was an issue published without at least one story on the unusual in the usual happenings of the community.

While Gwen liked practically everyone and seemed to me to make no effort whatever to discriminate between people I might want as friends and those I would have kept at a polite distance, her quick wit on more than one occasion served to put someone in his place if he needed it and to win respect for her at the same time.

There was, for instance, her first—and last—close encounter with Fred McGuire, our competitor at the *Grundy County Missourian,* whom we had met our first day at the *Gazette.* The *Republican-Times* at Trenton and the *Princeton Post,* the weekly in the county seat of nearby Mercer County, were cooperative, even lending a Lino-type operator or equipment in a pinch, in spite of the fact that we sold advertising in both towns. McGuire, on the other hand, was frankly and gleefully out to put us in a spot and taunt us for being there.

Shortly after we came to the county, the Democrats decided to stage a political meeting called, in northwest Missouri, a "speaking." It was an off-year with no elec-tion coming, and not many such rallies were being held, but they had a speaker, and a number of people came from Trenton—including, of course, McGuire.

McGuire had practically dared us to cover the event, inferring that since we had a Republican paper we wouldn't be fair-minded enough to do so. As a matter of fact, we had every intention of covering the activities of both parties in news columns, a policy we felt was only game as well as good politics, confining our political views to a column that was my special precinct on the editorial page.

Knowing my radical Republicanism, Gwen was afraid I'd blow my top if I found myself in the enemy camp, so she persuaded me to let her attend the meeting and take along Edra, who was a Democrat, for company and possibly to introduce her to people whom she had not met. I pressed her navy silk seersucker dress, which had a pink organdy collar, and saw that she was dressed in her best, including my pink gloves, to be sure she would keep up her morale. Then I went to bed with a book.

She came home bubbling over. They had had their meeting, and during the chitchat afterward McGuire decided to have a little fun at my sister's expense. She took his first few references to her supposed alignment with the opposition with good grace—she didn't consider herself particularly partisan and was, in fact, I found later, a closet Democrat. She even passed over the insinuation that she was too young and inexperienced to run a newspaper. She had not forgotten, however, that she had been informed that he had said he would have us run out of the county within a year.

Several Trenton people came up and made her welcome, among them a woman doctor whom I had met a few weeks previously. She mentioned improvements we had been making on the *Gazette* and praised our intention to cover news of either party. Such cordiality toward his rival was too much for McGuire.

"I don't believe she is really a Republican," he put in. "Her sister may be, but I'll bet she is really a Democrat at heart."

"Well, really, Mr. McGuire," Gwen looked up at him, "I've never voted either ticket yet."

"Don't you Kansans consider it a duty to cast your vote?" he asked jeeringly, insinuating, she felt, that she was shirking the duty of a newspaper editor.

She just smiled sweetly, while her gaze fixed itself in a kind of fascination on the spot where the unshaded lightbulb reflected on his balding head. "Why of course, but isn't there a law in Missouri, too, that you have to be twenty-one before you are allowed to vote?" she inquired innocently.

Her shot in the dark had hit his Achilles' heel, and

McGuire, who was at least fortyish and trying to ignore his receding hairline and developing bay window, reddened at the laughter that swept over the crowd and suddenly found himself without an answer. He never played in her alley again at public meetings.

Gwen wouldn't be satisfied until she had tried out everything in the shop. I was horrified when she began feeding the job press, for I had heard of mutilating accidents in such work. I couldn't even stand to watch her.

"Don't be silly," she exploded. "I'm not going to put my hand in and get it smashed. People who get hurt on job presses do it grabbing for paper. They get careless. If I miss a sheet I'll just let it go. It's only a sheet of paper."

With her sense of rhythm and fine coordination, she developed into an excellent press feeder, and her calmness kept her from having any accidents.

Regardless of what the situation was, she was always there first. At two o'clock one December morning that first winter we were awakened by a neighbor calling under Gwen's window, "Gwendolyn, get up! The town's on fire!"

Because I liked to read very late, I'd been sleeping in a tiny room off the living room, which we had furnished with our books and a writing desk and dignified by calling it a den since it was small enough to heat with a portable oil heater.

We were both up instantly and rushed to the kitchen window. A faint red glow reflecting above the snow-covered rooftops was visible in the direction of the business district. A horrible gone sensation lodged in the pit of my stomach. "Our insurance on the *Gazette* just covers the mortgage," my mind ran.

The shop was in the basement of a brick building on the west side of the street under Pete Taylor's department store. "Pete Taylor's one of our best advertisers," I thought desperately.

On the east side of the street at the opposite corner were our two other best advertisers, Wilson's Grocery and Dennis Drugstore, both in neat brick buildings, and the small brick office of the capable local dentist, Dr. Heck. Beyond that was a row of frame buildings stretching to the next corner. A blaze starting in one of those buildings, given a north wind, would sweep the whole block before it. Fed on the frame structures, dry as tinder, it would gain such headway that Spickard's volunteer fire department with practically nonexistent water pressure might find it impossible to save even the brick buildings on the south corner.

"I don't think it's the shop," Gwen said practically, shedding flannel pajamas on her way back to her bedroom. "It's too far north." She dashed into wool slacks, put on a heavy sweater under her coat because it was so cold, slipped into her flat-heeled shoes so she could run, tied a scarf around her head, and in almost no time was at the scene.

Some minutes later I appeared, completely dressed with my glasses and lipstick. By that time the fire, in a plumbing shop two doors away from the *Gazette,* was sufficiently under control that we could be reasonably certain it would not spread. The volunteers played a thin stream of water over the adjoining buildings as a precautionary measure. In Spickard you didn't expect to put out a fire. You just kept it from spreading if you could.

The crowd began to chat, and someone commented

on the state of dress and undress of the spectators, including those who had remembered their glasses. "Do you wear lipstick to bed?" I was teased.

Gwen justified her apparel, and I explained that I had hoped the fire wasn't at the *Gazette,* but even if it had been, I couldn't have done anything about it by being there a few minutes earlier. As for the glasses, I might have seen the fire without them, but I certainly would have snubbed any acquaintances who might have been across the street from me. I never tried to explain the lipstick. After several years in college and teaching, it was just a way of life when I appeared before the public.

Our reactions were typical of both of us. We both thought quickly and acted on logical reasoning, but her greater curiosity and her reporter's instinct made it imperative for her to be at the center of activity. I was still the perfectionist, even when the town was on fire.

If the combination of our opposite characteristics resulted in the paper being more newsy and also more accurate, it was inevitable that there would be times when we would not see things alike. We never quarreled over money—not that we had enough to perpetrate a good fight—because we both adhered to agreements we had made in the beginning to keep our financial relationships on a business basis and because we both abhorred pettiness. Nor was there any rivalry between us for personal recognition or any personal jealousy of the other's achievements. Had I done anything spectacular, she would have been sincerely happy about it. She is one of the most generous persons I have ever known. And while I sometimes wondered if I would ever work my way far enough through the mass of detail to obtain the practice in creative writing I had hoped for when we decided to go into the newspaper business, I could see no point in bungling a story she could do well. We each had to contribute the thing we could do best; the welfare of the *Gazette* came first.

Our disagreements usually grew out of our different work methods, my ambitions for her, and my desire to protect her from disappointments every young person faces. As a child I soaked up responsibility the way a sponge does water. When my mother admonished me to look after my little sister, I took it seriously. But my little sister had grown up and didn't want to be protected. She liked people the way they were, and whether or not they had a college degree or my definition of a future meant nothing to her. While our own futures might not have looked so bright to the casual bystander, there was never any real doubt in my mind or hers—even when things were blackest and I would remark grimly, "Well, if necessary we can always go back to teaching school"—that our newspaper venture would eventually be a success. We stubbornly refused to admit we could be licked. Gwen always said we wouldn't know if we were. We would think of something.

I wanted to work on the *Gazette* day and night. Gwen liked time off to be with people just for fun. She did things so much more easily and quickly than I; it seemed to me that if she would only put forth the time and effort I did she would be able to go far, but she just laughed at the idea that she could develop her talent my way, and went on doing things her own way. I didn't understand then that her interest in people was the underlying factor in her ability to find news in the small town routine of Spickard. Nor did I understand her wanting to do things just for the enjoyment she derived from them. She had fun making interviews and weaving stories.

My complete inability to recognize a joke and her love of teasing accentuated the situation. One day during the political campaign she breezed in, dropped into her chair, and announced, "Well, I hear another of your legal eagles is running for prosecuting attorney. This one's a Democrat—popular, might win, too."

"Legal eagles," I frowned. "What -c-?"

"Lawyer, of course," she explained impatiently.

"Gwen, I don't think that's very respectful," I began severely. "Jack Hoover [the Republican candidate] is definitely a very personable person, and I'm sure . . ."

"Oh, sure," Gwen interrupted. "Sure. He's fine. All lawyers are if they are Republicans. You never thought I might be insulting a Democrat, too. You, my dear, are definitely politically prejudiced. This Democrat might be the better man . . ."

"I'm not prejudiced," I insisted. "I believe in party loyalty."

I sat back and prepared to convince her that I was not prejudiced, that Jack Hoover had the support of the party leadership because he was capable, when a horrible thought struck me.

"Say, who is this Democrat?" I asked. "I don't know any Democratic lawyers in Grundy County who might run . . ."

"Oh, I don't remember his name," she shrugged. "They say he's very popular."

"You don't remember his name!" I exploded. "Well for heaven's sake how can you disregard an important thing . . ." I broke off suddenly, aware her mouth was twitching, her eyes dancing.

"You made it all up!" I accused hotly.

"Got a raise, didn't I?" she laughed. "The moral, my

dear editor, is, Don't take your politics so seriously. They might bite."

Frequently she exaggerated something she knew I wouldn't approve of just to "get a raise" out of me, and she usually got it. I forgot she had the welfare of the paper at heart as much as I did and that in matters of consequence she exercised sound judgment. I hadn't learned that no two people want exactly the same things and that the same pattern of action would have been as bad a misfit for us so far as our happiness was concerned as each other's clothes. She was doing her best to make me less serious, but she seldom succeeded.

There were many pleasant experiences to remember from living and working together, however. As the "editor girls" we were invited to several social functions right at the start that helped us to get acquainted. The supply of "desirable" men (at least in my estimation) was practically nil—most young unmarried men were at least attached—but there were several girls working in the two banks or teaching in the grade school or high school whom we found congenial.

I always looked to Gwen, though, to arrange our get-togethers, whether it was a trip in Nancy to see a movie in Trenton or a waffle supper in our little house with cottage cheese and olives as well as traditional toppings. She had a flair for finding new things to do or thinking up ways to do old things differently.

Although we lived on a limited budget, our meals were never monotonous. Gwen declared I knew about only two meats, lunch meat and hamburger, but she more than made up for my deficiencies. With no apparent effort whatever and with no cooperation from our temperamental kerosene stove, she could whip up a lemon pie that would melt in your mouth, and with the same ease prepare a meal for a whole group if we wanted to entertain at Sunday dinner and still leave us sufficient grocery funds for the rest of the week. It was surprising how far a pound of round steak would go when she cubed it, braised it with brown gravy, and served it over mashed potatoes. Her salads, tossed together with leftover vegetables, rivaled any chef's.

Her bran hot rolls were out of this world. She gave a lesson in preparing them to a friend who married a young doctor after several years of teaching country school. The first batch turned out perfectly, and like any bride, Sally neglected to mention to her husband that she'd had assistance. Doc was so pleased he took some of the rolls downtown to show off his new wife's accomplishments to his men friends. After such a build-up Sally was afraid to try on her own, so Gwen kept her secret, helped her make the rolls, and let her take the credit. Sally soon gained sufficient skill and confidence to live up to her reputation.

Another of Gwen's specialties was chocolate cake, moist and delectable. That quiet young man named Orville, who by the time we were in our second winter at Spickard was becoming a frequent visitor at our house, was especially fond of chocolate cake, so perhaps it wasn't a coincidence that Gwen baked one nearly every Saturday morning and that by Monday there wasn't a crumb left. It was not unusual for a few others of the town's young people to drop in now and then, either.

Where political activity challenged my interest, church work took hers, and with characteristic lack of prejudice she became involved in the activities of both of the two largest churches, the Methodist and the Christian (Disciples of Christ). She sang in the choir for special programs, was available, regardless of what work she had ahead, to sing at funerals in any church, and with typical versatility would fill whatever spot was needed as a soloist or in a duet or quartet, singing either soprano or alto. I would sometimes accompany her on the piano for a violin solo.

Young people's church activities were a favorite with her, but she usually found time also to contribute a cake or pie to the food sales sponsored by women's groups, and fund-raisers were often for youth activities. She also liked to help serve fund-raiser dinners, sometimes necessary to pay the preacher his small salary. She took her church duties seriously, but she had fun with them and enjoyed her church work more than many people do.

She carefully gave publicity to all the churches in town impartially and went to any amount of trouble to get their notes in the paper each week in the belief that publicity would help the church and that many of the woes of people would vanish if they attended and worked in some church. She was often infuriated at the pettiness of some members, but after blowing off steam at home she would be right in there pitching again for a more effective church program.

"My work interferes with my hobbies," she complained after an especially strenuous week, but on top of her cooking, entertaining, music, and church activities, she still found time for writing copious letters to her scads of acquaintances, for reading the numerous magazines to which we subscribed at a discount by virtue of being in the publishing field, as well as the books we borrowed from the Trenton library, and for just sitting around "batting the breeze" with almost anyone who felt in a mood to talk.

There is no doubt she worried over finances, but she was always sure that as long as we kept working and didn't let anything get us down we'd be OK. Her faith might have been naive, even childlike, but she backed it up with sound planning, hard work, and a never-dimming zest for living. Occasionally when things piled up she "blew her top" in a sudden explosion of temper, or submitted briefly to a spell of blues, but usually a little stroke of luck, an unexpected pleasure, or even a few words of appreciation would snap her out of it and she would bounce back to her usual positive self again.

Chapter 7

How: Worrying and Figuring

Ardis

The weather proved a reasonably accurate barometer of the financial status of the *Grundy County Gazette*. When the sun shone and the moisture was right for crops, the farmers were in a hopeful frame of mind. Sometimes they even had a little cash. They came to town frequently, and the merchants advertised. If the weather was bad, the farmers stayed home and the business people looked upon advertising as an expense they could eliminate.

Unseasonable temperatures had a most peculiar effect on our advertisers. Their reaction to great extremes of heat, cold, rainfall, or drought I could understand, for all business depended on agriculture. Even Spickard's one payroll, the canning factory, required a good tomato season; otherwise the factory just didn't open. But perfectly delightful weather, if it wasn't the kind usually expected at the particular time of year, appeared to affect business almost as adversely as a grasshopper invasion.

Country newspapers flourish during some months, merely exist through others. The trick was to achieve sufficient surplus when the going was good to tide us over when it was not. After a year I learned when to expect a profit and when we would do well to manage to pay help, rent, and utilities. I also learned which accounts could be depended on to pay promptly as soon as we presented our statements on the first of the month, and which would be slow or doubtful. I learned not to sell more to those whose standing might be slightly shaky than they would be able to handle if their bills piled up enough before collection to frighten them.

After the paper was out for the last week before the first of the next month I would sit down grimly with the past four or five issues—some months have five Thursdays—and make up the statements. The set jaw and grim determination to see an unpleasant task through reflected my deep hatred of figures and my reluctance to come to grips with reality. I had omitted any math courses not absolutely required all through high school and college, and lack of practice made drudgery of keeping books.

When the statements and necessary records were completed, I would separate the accounts into groups: those I expected to pay us at once, those I knew would pay on the fifteenth, those that wouldn't pay until next month (legal publications often were not settled until after a sheriff's sale or at the close of a term of court), and finally, those that were slow and doubtful. Then I allotted our own bills in order of their urgency to definite groups of settlements.

Our first payments usually came from our three grocery stores and Schooler's Furniture Store. The rent was not due until the fifteenth, so it could wait on a utilities ad paid at that time. The electric bill had to be paid promptly. We always paid the telephone bill sometime during the current month, but since we were billed in advance for it anyway, it didn't worry me quite so much if it was a few days late, and no one ever threatened to take the phone out. A good long legal publication, billed by the line at legal rates, which were much better than those we received for display space, was a wonderful break and meant we could afford something we especially needed or wanted for the shop or even for ourselves.

March first was moving day for farmers. We always had a long front-page story about where different families had moved. Sometimes there would be a chain of families who all had to move at the same time because each family's moving hinged on the moving out of the preceding occupants. As soon as the moving job was completed, everyone started repairing fences and getting ready to plant spring crops. March was always a good month for advertising. Activity meant business for hardware, seed, and supply stores. The grocery stores came in for their share also as there were more people coming to town.

April also was good, especially if Easter came in April and if the weather was right for spring clothing. We usually managed to sell a few clothing ads every spring to Trenton firms who didn't advertise regularly. When two sisters, Cordie Wild and Nelle Keith, opened a ladies' dress and accessories shop in Spickard, they became regular advertisers. High school graduation meant new clothes for the graduates and other family members if they could afford them, and people were cheerful in

May. June was especially good as spring gave way to summer and weddings took place. Baby chicks grew into broilers and provided a little spendable income.

In July business dropped off abruptly. The weather usually became hot, and if the year brought a drought and grasshoppers as well, as happened at least twice, business took a nosedive. It wasn't too bad, though, for we sometimes received payment from legals at the close of the June term of court, and our own living expenses were at a minimum with no fuel to buy and the abundance of fresh vegetables given to us by friendly subscribers. August was dull, unless it was an election year, which is an answer to the country newspaper's prayers. What would a country newspaper have done in a monarchy?

If September opened with a cool, brisk breeze, we would be all set for a lively fall. School clothing, the winter's supply of coal, new heating equipment, new furniture to enjoy during the long months ahead—these were naturals for the sale of advertising, and we found sales were better if we were prepared to furnish copy suggestions for the hesitant. Young's Lumber Yard would remind people about preparing for winter by making necessary repairs. Grocery ads included canning supplies all summer and fall—sugar, Mason jars, lids, and other things.

Farmers marketed their crops in the fall, and if there was any cash around, it was at that time. The canning factory payroll put some money into circulation. October was our best month for cash subscriptions. Our first October in Spickard really saw us doing a big subscription business as farmer after farmer came in to pay for two or three—or sometimes as many as four—years back and pay up for another year with the remark, "I intended to stop the paper but we like it so much better we don't want to be without it." That was almost as much music to our ears as the jingle of cash.

November was only slightly less prosperous than October, and December, bringing Christmas, was something we looked forward to eagerly. Selecting the best week for advertisers of Christmas merchandise, we would double the size of the paper, print extra copies (postal regulations permitted sending the paper to everyone in the trade territory three times a year for the purpose of obtaining new subscribers), and sell additional advertising. We always made money in December.

After the first year we learned to keep enough of December's bounty available to carry us through January and February, when we would take in just about enough to cover office expenses and payroll. North Missouri winters were severe; the country roads became impassable at times, and activities just stopped. Even news was scarce, except for obituaries and stories of funerals. Bears must have had north Missouri weather in mind when they instituted hibernation.

We had one break, though. Living in Spickard was not expensive. The best rental housing in town, a bungalow with running water, was ten dollars a month. It was already occupied, so we rented a cottage that was not "modern," partitioned off an enclosed back porch we didn't need, and sent to a mail-order house for chemical plumbing. This seemed to cause some concern to one of our neighbors, for she confided to Mrs. Farmer, the Methodist minister's wife, who lived across the street from us, that she had never seen us making trips to the dilapidated structure at the back of the lot and didn't know how we managed. Mrs. Farmer assured her we were perfectly normal. Mrs. Farmer was always popping in with hot biscuits, cookies, or something from the big garden Mr. Farmer raised, and with friendly encouragement. What she didn't tell was that we usually took care of the sanitation shift in the dark of night. Chemical toilets do not connect to sewers, so it was just as well that the original facility was still in the backyard.

We made all of our own dresses and suits. Major clothing items, such as a winter coat, we bought in the after-Christmas or pre-Easter sales, locally if we could, or on our occasional much looked forward to trips to Kansas City. There was one item that needed to be replaced more often, though, and that exception almost caused a minor domestic calamity. Gwen had long, beautifully shaped legs and slender ankles. I often quipped that she should model hose instead of just wearing them out. She would come in from selling ads, sit down at the rough table that served as her desk, stretch out her legs, and pop would go another pair. I could get along with one pair for six or eight weeks, sometimes longer, but practically every Saturday she had to have a dollar for more hose.

"It looks as though you're going to have to get an extra advertiser and consign his money to paying for your hose," I remarked tartly one day when we had just finished paying for a six months' supply of newsprint and were especially short.

There was a Spickard feed dealer—we'll call him McDougle—whose Scottish characteristics were not confined to his name. He hadn't liked the former editor, and he didn't believe in advertising. One warm summer afternoon after being out an unusually long time Gwen came in triumphantly waving a piece of paper. "Here's my hose money for two whole weeks," she declared, throwing it on my desk.

I picked it up and looked at it. It was copy for an advertisement, two columns by five inches at twenty cents an inch, for a cost of two dollars. For anyone in Spickard except the grocery stores and the furniture store, this was doing all right. The signature was McDougle.

"I can't believe it!" I exclaimed. "I thought he didn't believe in advertising. What did you do, hypnotize him?"

"Oh, I just perched myself on his counter and crossed my legs and sat there until he gave it to me," she flipped, hoisting herself on her desk and illustrating.

I noticed the tailored blue cotton dress that was a perfect example of what the suitably clothed country editor should wear and the high-heeled navy pumps she usually saved for special occasions. I recalled my catty remarks about her hose money, and my conscience took a terrible turn. She was my younger sister and I was responsible for her. We had never asked favors because we were a couple of girls trying to make it on our own. We had always sold on merit—what an ad could do for an advertiser. Now, just because I couldn't curb my vicious tongue, my sister was playing up to a silly old man for a couple of dollars.

"Now, look here," I exploded, "if we can't sell advertising on the basis of what it is worth, we'd better go back to teaching school. We don't want business on a personal basis. I wouldn't have anyone think for a moment that either of us is trading on the fact that we are young and alone in the world and feel they have to help us out. We'll make our living the hard way—by working for it," I lectured.

"Don't be silly," she replied, flexing a shapely ankle. "This is the hard way. These high heels are killing me." Her eyes were twinkling.

Then I remembered the wonderful letters she used

to write—about a scene in that matchbox schoolhouse, or baking a cake, or playing with a dance orchestra at a neighborhood party. I remembered one of the reasons I had put my savings into the *Grundy County Gazette,* and I relaxed. Gwen would always make a good story out of any incident, even if it was only about selling a two-dollar ad to a stoop-shouldered old man with a terrible walk and ninety-nine cents out of the first and every succeeding dollar he had ever gotten his hands on. She was quite capable of handling the situation if he had a yen to get his hands on her, too. He probably received a ten-dollar sales talk on what a good ad would do for him, and a friendly grin that lifted his spirits, but I knew that was all.

We might not always agree, but on one thing we stood pat. From the first we maintained a policy of no liquor advertising. For a time it meant a loss of badly needed revenue, but gradually we built up enough business from those who approved of that policy to offset the loss. I had only to remember the explanation I gave the distributor who offered ads, and Gwen's sharp agreement with me when he insisted, to be certain that we stood together in maintaining the principles on which our business decisions were based.

This was the Bible Belt in 1935, six decades ago. It seems like more than a century.

Chapter 8

How: Horse Trading, Hired Help, Helping Out, and High Heels

Gwen

The first issues of the *Gazette* will always be associated inseparably in my mind with Kes and Edra. Gradually our wings dried and we flew in our own newspaper direction more and more, but while we were starting Kes and Edra played a vital part in those first few struggling, thrilling, uncertain days.

What we would have done without Kes, our reliable if temperamental printer-operator who assumed, at first, full responsibility for the back shop, I shudder to think. He was about fifteen years older than I, had been married, divorced, and disillusioned, and made it clear that while he enjoyed the company of women, no girl need get serious about him as marrying again was definitely not for him. As far as I know, he held out the rest of his life, although he was the supercharged sort of man with a fatal attraction for girls who threw themselves at him in spite of the fact he made it no secret they did so at their own risk. Part of his attraction, I suppose, lay in his making them responsible for their own actions and letting them know he considered himself under no obligation to them. He was, however, fair-minded and did not take advantage.

Kes and Ardis, both of whom would rather give than take orders, clashed frequently, and although neither said much, the air was often charged with tension. I attempted to act as arbitrator, and since Kes took the time and patience to teach me everything he could about the mechanical side of printing, I was appreciative and grateful and tried to let him know it. Consequently, we got along fine. I might have been tempted to engage in a mild flirtation once in a while because of the challenge he presented to women to see if they could change his mind, but I didn't dare incur my sister's wrath, and I wisely refrained, knowing I was no match for his disenchanted and sophisticated outlook on life. Kes was enough of a gentleman that he would not have made the first advances to someone in the same office, even though he must have known that the idea of my being "boss" seemed a little silly even to me. I behaved as I supposed I should, and managed to keep peace in the print shop. We remained good friends, and I was glad for him when, after nearly a year, he was offered a job he couldn't refuse, although I hated to see him leave.

Occasionally Kes would be offered a few days work for the Rock Island Railroad, for which he had dispatched trains before the depression. These offers meant too much for him financially for him to turn them down, and his sudden departures sometimes put us in an awful spin, but he always managed to get the paper out. He would never give us any assurance that he would be back in time, but he always was. That was typical of him.

Only after he left and we went through a series of inefficient help did we fully appreciate Kes. He took responsibility without question; avidly respected deadlines, accuracy, and shop confidences; and applauded originality. He cooperated completely with our new ideas and offered suggestions of his own for improvements. Even though we might have felt like beating him when (rarely) he refused to put in a late ad after the page forms were closed (with the makeup completed, any changes were a lot of trouble and caused delay), we realized that his influence on the *Grundy County Gazette* was good and that he was a better man than he pretended to be.

Our other "help," Edra, had reported for the *Gazette* for five years. She had no training and little talent for writing and was of use only until we got acquainted enough to handle the work ourselves. Knowing everybody and everything about Spickard, she, without knowing it, often kept me from making an embarrassing error by telling me a bit of gossip that kept me from linking names together in a story when to do so would have been inappropriate. Edra and Kes, because of personal loyalties to friends on the opposite sides of a divorce case and because of differences in their personalities, were at each other's throats half the time. Again I tried to arbitrate, but who could arbitrate successfully between an intelligent, strictly honest, attractive, and confessedly disillusioned man and an impulsive, warmhearted girl whose nature sometimes made her treat the truth so lightly that the results were disastrous. Whatever debt she compiled from the troubles her actions caused herself or others should have been marked paid long since, however, for pay she did later over a period of years in personal tragedies that could inspire only pity even in her enemies.

We were trying to think of some way to inform her we no longer needed her, knowing the tiny salary she was getting was all she had. Then one day she solved the problem for us. It was press day, and I noticed she stumbled a couple of times as she attempted to mount the platform we stood on to feed the newsprint onto the cylinder of Old Bertha that would roll it over the form for printing. I didn't think much about it until she missed the first sheet, causing Kes to have to clean the torn paper off and start up again. When she missed the second sheet, she giggled, "There must be something wrong—they just don't go in." I caught her as she nearly toppled off the platform and said gently, "Go home, Edra." I knew Kes was at the point of exploding, so I hopped up and fed the press myself as I had done often before. I didn't miss a sheet. I knew Edra sometimes drank, but I never had detected it at work before. Shortly after that incident she resigned and returned to the job for which she had trained, that of a beautician.

I liked Edra for her friendly qualities, but it was a relief when she decided to quit. I had attempted unsuccessfully to teach her how to write a social item, or an obituary, with some regard for the rules of journalism. She did far better in her chosen field.

It became the usual for people to express surprise when either of us was introduced as one of the new *Gazette* editors. A couple of months after we started, Jim Price, the editor of the *Princeton Post*, called us with an SOS. Princeton, as did many small towns, had an annual celebration with all sorts of activities, including a

Most Beautiful Baby show. Infants were scrutinized by a panel of judges who chose three winners, usually to the chagrin of the mothers of the nonwinners.

"Our baby show is at two o'clock this afternoon," Jim said, sounding a little harried, "and we don't have any judges. We need people who don't know the families so no one can be accused of favoritism. Could one of you help us out?"

I had answered the phone and, without asking, knew this was my assignment. I loved babies and could never wait to pick up any who happened to be around, whereas Ardis preferred to view them from a respectable distance. "Sure," I agreed. Jim had been a good friend to us from the start, even rescuing us once by printing an edition when we had a mechanical problem. I was glad to reciprocate.

"Ray Van Meter will pick you up on the way, about one o'clock," Jim went on. Ray Van Meter was business manager of the *Trenton Republican-Times*. Spickard was halfway between Trenton and Princeton. The *Republican-Times* was friendly, too. I wondered why on earth an old bachelor—he must have been all of thirty-five—would be asked to judge a baby show, but decided perhaps it was a desperation measure.

I rushed home, put on my navy seersucker dress with its big pink collar, an outfit I had designed and made myself, grabbed my wide-brimmed navy hat, grimaced as I thought how my feet would feel after an afternoon of standing on those high heels, and borrowed Ardis's pink gloves. People dressed up for an occasion in those days.

At Princeton, Jim gave us our instructions. "Take plenty of time," he cautioned. "Look at them all several times. When you do decide, line them up to the front of the platform and make the presentations." He handed us ribbons and certificates that would allow them to collect $5.00 for first place, $3.00 for second, and $2.00 for third. Then he introduced us.

"This is Miss Hamilton," he said, "one of the new editors who bought the *Gazette* at Spickard recently, and Mr. Van Meter of the *Trenton Republican-Times.*"

We dutifully followed instructions and finally made our choices. "You make the announcements and I'll give them the prizes," Ray suggested.

"Coward," I thought. "I'll fix you. I don't want to be hated by those nonwinning mothers any more than you do."

I stepped to the front and began. "These babies are all so adorable I wanted to give them all first prize, but Mr. Van Meter insists we have to make some choices, so here are the winners." I gave Ray what I hoped was a dazzling smile, and we made the presentations.

As we were leaving I overheard one of the ladies say, "That girl is an editor? She looks too young." Maybe that is why we escaped unscathed. Ardis and I both met with the "too young" evaluation several times. Going home in the car that evening I secretly slipped off my shoes. I was glad it was dark. My feet were resenting bitterly the sacrifice I had made them undertake so I could be the well-dressed editor.

We had a lot of fun with our paper that first year in spite of its always precarious financial footing. One time the bank account got down to seventy-three cents, which really isn't much on which to operate a business and meet even a small payroll, let alone live. Ardis insisted she had to keep the books—all of the financial stuff—so I let her do most of the worrying about how to pay the bills and divide up what money we could get our hands on, and I concentrated on how we could sell more advertising, job printing, and subscriptions. I reminded the businesspeople regularly that we printed letterheads, envelopes, statements, cards, sale bills, and anything else they might need. The job printing department often saved the day for us, and during an election year when candidates used cards and other printing, it was a real bonus. Of course the election ballots, which were divided up among all the papers with job printing departments in the county, were gravy.

If we could have paid the bills with the words of praise our subscribers bestowed on our willing heads, we would have had no worries. People did seem to like the paper. The trouble was that there just wasn't much cash money in 1935. We figured that if we could find a way more country people could pay for a subscription, we could increase the circulation enough to sell more advertising in Trenton and larger ads in Spickard. We tried to sell only to Trenton businesses that were not competitive with Spickard merchants.

As soon as we felt we had made several improvements, we sent a sample copy of the *Grundy County Gazette* to every home in Spickard and along the rural mail routes, and we made every effort to make that issue as interesting and as appealing as we possibly could. We continued this practice as often as postal regulations allowed, three times a year, usually in November for Christmas, in March for spring, and perhaps in August or September. It wasn't long before we found that many nonsubscribers wanted the local paper, but they just didn't have any money. Grasshopper invasions, drought, resulting crop failures, the depression, and low prices were all fingers on the hand that choked off ready cash. However, we learned that when a Missourian wants anything, there is a way of getting it besides buying. It's called horse trading. We soon found ourselves doing a regular horse-trading business—subscriptions for almost anything. In a short time we caught on—they had more respect for us if we drove a hard bargain.

Now, with steaks and chops selling for $2.00 to at least $5.00 a pound, I reminisce lovingly about a telephone conversation I carried on one cold January day in 1936. There was a dismal sheet of ice over everything, making ad selling a difficult job, and business was at an all-time low. Then the phone rang.

"Is this the *Gazette*?" a man's voice asked.

"Yes, it is," I replied.

"I want the paper a year and my subscription is already three years behind. Would you take a quarter of beef?"

A beautiful vision of steaks and roasts for the rest of the winter arose before me, but the heritage of my Scottish ancestors and all my Yankee thrift came to the fore and told me not to sound too eager.

"A hindquarter?" I bargained.

"Sure," the voice held the amused respect of one good trader for another. Besides, he had plenty of beef and I had plenty of subscriptions. As another subscriber put it, they were plowing under pigs in Washington. I had helped my mother and father cut up and can beef too many times not to know what I wanted.

"OK," I said. "Bring it in." Two hours later, I, as chief cook, was wondering what on earth I was going to do with what looked like a huge amount of top-quality beef for which I had paid four dollars' worth of subscriptions. I cut it into manageable pieces, wrapped it carefully, and kept it on the enclosed back porch, where it froze solid until I got it canned. It fed us all winter along with a cured ham, a side of bacon, and some other things I acquired the same way. The sight of all that meat gave us almost as secure a feeling as money in the bank.

Another time a quite astonishing lady popped into the shop. She seemed to have the energy of a steam engine, and although she was scrupulously clean, her clothes were well worn and her hair was wildly wind-blown. She held out a plump, dressed fryer.

"This," she announced loudly, "is worth about thirty-five cents. I'll bring you one every Saturday for the next three weeks and then you can send me the paper."

"I'll start it next week," I promised. So for the next four Sundays straight we feasted on fried chicken. Such bartering was not advised by our journalism professors in college, but we doubted if they ever ran a country newspaper, and at least we built up a lot of valuable goodwill, never went hungry, and increased the sub-scription list substantially.

We seldom had to buy eggs. We had all sorts of gar-den vegetables and fruit in season. Whenever someone raised a big tomato, potato, or peach, they made a pres-ent of it to the "*Gazette* girls." It was understood there would be a "piece in the paper" about it the next week. On one occasion I had a bad sinus attack that kept me from work for a day or so and from functioning prop-erly while I was there, and left Ardis with so much to do she forgot a significant gift, bringing down the wrath of the stalwart individual who was sure his sweet po-tato set an all-time record for size. He came into the shop demanding in no uncertain tones to know why he didn't get a story when so and so had had one on his corn.

"Oh, we thought this was so unusual we wanted to have a picture of you with the potato," I assured him. "I'll take a picture and we will have a cut made so we can print it." A cut was a metal engraving used to print a picture in the paper.

I borrowed a camera from Frances Brown, wife of the druggist M. I. Brown and co-owner with him of their drugstore; she always kept a camera handy to record pictures of their beautiful little daughter. I bought the film from the drugstore, took the picture, and went to the trouble of getting a cut. The result pleased the man so much he made us a gift of a bushel of sweet potatoes. The only problem was sweet potatoes are not my favorite food. I managed to trade part of them for something else I liked better—I think it was apples. Country editors in the 1930s had to be quick-witted, have a sense of humor and a big imagination, and be absolutely undiscriminating about the publicity of local affairs. Those little local items formed the vertebrae of goodwill a newspaper built in a community, and the influence and the success of the paper depended on the strength of those vertebrae.

It was fun to be invited to all the social functions of the community, too, and it was understood that we were not to bring anything to the covered-dish luncheons. I loved to cook, so I usually did, but I knew I was expected to give the affair a "write-up." Besides, a few free meals made up for the few subscriptions or small bills we failed to collect. Also, those ladies cooked their best; their piecrusts (made with lard) flaked to the touch of a fork, and their cakes were so light you almost had to hold them down to eat them. I don't know why I ever thought I could produce food like theirs, but I tried.

We never went cold, either. One day someone called and said, "Will you take a rick of wood for a subscription?"

"A rick?" I asked. My Kansas background had educated me in no such term. "How much is a rick?"

I had expected an explanation in relation to a cord, which I would have understood at least vaguely.

"Oh, I'll give you your money's worth for a dollar," the voice assured me.

"OK. Take it to our house and I'll meet you there with a receipt for your subscription," I promised.

At the house I stared with astonishment at the amount of wood in our shed, enough to supply our German heater for weeks. I traded ricks or racks of wood all winter and never got the same amount twice, but it was always such an ample amount that it was more than my money's worth. At the time I thought perhaps they were taking pity on my youth and ignorance, but I have since decided the farmers of that community hold a record for generosity.

Incidentally, that German heater definitely was a foreigner as far as we were concerned. I never came to a satisfactory understanding with it, and it left me with a complex about stoves that makes me shudder at the sight of one. Out of necessity I learned quickly how to bargain with those expert Missouri horse traders, but nothing in my Scottish, English, Irish, Kansas pioneer heritage had taught me how to cope with that stubborn, headstrong, obstinate German heater.

Chapter 9

A Godfather for the Gazette

Ardis

The winter of 1935–1936 was one of the most severe on
record. It began on Christmas day with a sudden drop
in temperature from "seasonable" to zero in the course
of a few hours. Gwen had gone home on the bus for
Thanksgiving and the following Sunday had driven back
with our favorite aunt, Miss Lizzie Hanna, who was to
visit us until after the holidays. For something different,
we decided to have our Christmas dinner in Gallatin at
Mrs. MacDonald's tearoom, famous all over the state for
its delicious chicken dinners and its hospitality. We
planned to leave home around noon. Lucille Coon,
who worked at the Bank of Spickardsville and was halfway between Gwen and me in age, was going with us.

The wind was rising when we walked to Terry's garage on the highway, where we kept my car and Aunt
Lizzie's car since our place had no shelter for a car and
the street-rocking project had not yet been completed. I
don't know why we didn't take Nancy, since she had a

wonderful heater right under the feet of the driver; but Aunt Lizzie was always generous and liked to do things for us, and she insisted that we go in her Whippet. It didn't have a heater, and the north wind was an icy blast when we drove back against it after a leisurely meal. Gwen and I both froze our feet on the way and were in acute misery when we finally arrived home to find that the fire had gone out, there was ice in the water bucket in the kitchen, and our houseplants had frozen in the living room.

Fortified by her long experience on a Kansas farm, Aunt Lizzie took over the firemaking and coaxed the German heater into a semblance of compliance while Gwen succumbed to a rare attack of homesickness and I gritted my teeth and resigned myself to another winter that was to surpass by far anything northern Kansas had produced in the three years I had spent there. Obviously, the former editor wanted to sell his paper when he assured me the north Missouri climate was not too severe. I couldn't blame him for moving to New Mexico— the warmer part, I observed.

The temperature, however, did not stay at zero for long. Instead, it dropped to twenty-four below and remained at that point for six weeks except for occasional days when it warmed up, say to ten or fifteen below. To make things worse, the building housing the *Gazette* was sold and we were given notice to move. A basement was a necessity, since there wasn't a building in town with a floor strong enough to hold our four-ton press—which was small, as newspaper presses went. We finally found a basement under the drugstore operated by M. I. Brown and his wife. Their beautiful three-year-old daughter, Beverly, with her black hair, blue eyes, and alert mind, was a great favorite among the gang of younger people who gathered frequently at the drugstore for sodas and companionship. We would have less space than at the former location, but Kes figured out how we could get everything in, and we hoped our new quarters would be less barnlike and easier on the fuel bill than those we were leaving.

It was only eight below on the day we moved, January 23. The work was planned for Friday, just after an issue was out, so we would have a few days to get the machinery adjusted before starting the next week's publication. Disregarding our inner voices, which told us they were not equal to the job, we hired two local men who had moved houses and other buildings some time in the past and possessed machinery for moving heavy equipment. Neither of them knew anything about a Linotype or a press, but they were to work under Kes's direction, and we thanked our lucky stars he treated the Linotype "machine" as though it were his own.

I didn't dare look when they took out the top-heavy Linotype. I was sure they would break it at any moment, but they got it through the door without too much trouble and started up the alley with it. I felt thoroughly helpless and completely superfluous, but it was so cold we could do nothing but sit around the heat register in the drugstore and get an occasional report on the progress. At four o'clock Kes came in and told us the Linotype was safe in its new place but the men had decided it was too cold to finish moving Old Bertha, the big press, that night and had left it in the alley. I hit the ceiling.

"Where are they?" I asked. "I think I'll go right now and give them a piece of my mind."

"I wouldn't advise you to," he cautioned, and if there was just a flicker of amusement somewhere he kept it well under control. "They're up at Ashbrook's garage, but they're in no condition to be reasoned with by this time. I took the rollers off and everything else that could be removed. It's covered, and it can't hurt it any to sit out overnight."

We dry-state Kansans still weren't used to thinking in terms of living where warming refreshments were readily available with or without the excuse of severe weather or a bad cold. It turned out our machinery was none the worse for our harrowing experience, and we soon felt quite at home in our new quarters, even though they were somewhat dingy and crowded.

The only virtue of the winter of 1936 was the wonderful relief that heralded the arrival of spring. The sun came out and melted the snow. Water rushed down the hills in torrents, and the streets became bottomless quagmires. A great peace engulfed me as, in winter coats and galoshes, we walked down to Otto Hamilton's combination insurance office and carpenter shop to attend the Franklin Township Republican convention. Otto, to whom we quickly disclaimed any relationship, was noted for his caustic tongue and his hardheadedness.

The purpose of the meeting was to name delegates to the county convention to be held in Trenton the following Saturday. Although Spickard was mainly Republican and all the businessmen except one were Republicans, there were very few people present. Someone suggested one of us as delegates, and Gwen, knowing how much it would mean to me, generously withdrew by saying truthfully that I had planned to go anyway to cover the event for the paper. I didn't find out until several years later that Gwen had eventually registered as a Democrat.

Saturday was one of those rare days of perfect sunshine that make one glad to be alive. I had several errands before the convention at two o'clock, so wearing a purple knitted dress I had bought with Dad's Christmas check and a new lavender hat that went well with my brown coat and accessories and feeling in quite a holiday mood, I drove down in the morning, collected on several bills, and even indulged in a bit of shopping at the dime store, where for twenty-five cents I bought a big cluster of violets to complete my outfit.

My most important mission I left to the last. For the past several months we had been carrying advertising from a pharmacy in New York, but the firm had failed to pay anything on account; finally tumbling to the fact that perhaps they didn't intend to pay, I had written to the Missouri Press Association to inquire into their credit rating. J. Edward Gerald, who was then the Press Association secretary, had replied promptly that other newspapers were having the same difficulty and had suggested that I place the matter in the hands of an attorney. The banker at Spickard thought perhaps L. A. Warden of Trenton would undertake to collect the amount on a commission basis.

Business interviews were still new to me, and I always experienced stage fright when I had to call on anyone about anything important. It was with a mixture of timidity and anticipation that I gave my name to the secretary, who returned in a moment to say Mr. Warden would see me. As I entered his office, I found myself looking way up at a big, broad-shouldered man who crossed the room to shake hands, seated me in his most comfortable chair, found me a footstool—all chairs are too high for me—and insisted that I take off my coat, which I did gratefully, since the temperature had risen so rapidly I was uncomfortably warm, although I wondered if it was correct to take one's coat off in a business office—all so quietly that in a very few minutes I was perfectly at ease.

He called in his secretary and dictated a collection letter. She returned almost immediately to ask whether *Gazette* had one *t* or two. I couldn't help remarking how difficult it was to obtain competent help and how much trouble Edra's inefficiency and Kes's ability to dispatch trains had caused us, and soon we were talking as though we had known each other all our lives.

He told me about his three children in college: Philip, who would graduate from the school of journalism at the University of Missouri that spring; Rebecca, who was to get her degree there in English; and the baby, Jessie, in Trenton junior college. I mentioned our University of Kansas background and our ambition to write, and from that day on the *Gazette* had a godfather who was a continual source of encouragement, inspiration, and plain, practical help. When I took my leave, he showed me through his law library, which I later learned was one of the finest in that section of the state.

That first day it seemed to me he knew everyone in Spickard, and I was not far wrong. Nor was I wrong in my impression that he was one of the kindest persons I had ever known, for that summer when I took over the Trenton ad beat and made frequent trips there to sell, collect, or attend a political meeting, he made me welcome at his office, and I discovered he would go out of his way at any time to help anyone, young or old, and that he especially enjoyed giving a lift to a young person trying to get a start.

Sometimes I felt that I took up too much of his time and would resolve to stay away. But as I made my rounds of business firms that might possibly have an ad or some job printing for us, he was sure to run across me somewhere and suggest that I come in when I had finished. Often he would have a tip for a news story or an idea where we might obtain some new business. He would tell me about his son, who had gone to work for the *Kansas City Packer,* and I would tell him my current problem. It certainly wasn't a fair exchange, but it was a wonderful break for the *Gazette* and one small editor, who will ever be eternally grateful.

Gradually, as we became better acquainted, I pieced many incidents together and could see the wealth of experiences and the philosophy that resulted in this understanding person. Reared on a Mercer County farm, he had put himself through a preparatory school at Cameron by working on a bridge gang, a job requiring great physical strength; then he had gone on to the University of Missouri, where he lived on beans and canned tomatoes, tended furnaces, operated a dry cleaning plant and later a real estate business, and played on the football team while getting his law degree.

He never forgot a face. He loved children, and if anyone with two or three little tots came into his office, he would start talking with the children the first thing. There was a big sign in his reception room that said in large black letters, "Fees for Consultation," but I've often wondered just what proportion of the "consultations" resulted in fees. It takes a healthy income to keep three children in college at one time, and his practice was extensive; but certainly I would not begin to estimate the number of elderly persons whom he helped with little if any remuneration or the young people to whom he offered encouragement or perhaps a letter of introduction or a word to the right person to help them along. He became our best press agent, and his suggestions on which firms were good for credit and which bills should be collected before they became too large in those depression days were invaluable.

It's a pleasure to record that his three children thoroughly justified his faith in them, for, when still young, they were all outstanding in their chosen fields. Philip became a Washington correspondent for the *Chicago Tribune*. Both daughters obtained master's degrees. Rebecca taught successfully in high schools for several years before her marriage, and Jessie, the younger girl, earned a Ph.D. and taught in universities. Nor would the story be complete without mention of the seven grandchildren—Philip's daughter and two sons; Rebecca's two daughters and two sons—for this is the story of a man who never passed a child in the street or saw one in a restaurant without noticing him or her and who had great confidence in the younger generation.

The *Gazette* never did collect the bill from the New York pharmacy, and later the Missouri Press Association reported that the firm had been indicted for using the mails to defraud. We didn't feel too bad, though. After all, what's fifty dollars compared with a godfather for your favorite child? Gwen in a practical moment remarked that the legal advice alone was probably worth far more than the amount we had lost on the pharmacy advertising.

Chapter 10

Politicking

Ardis

The wife of one of the successful candidates had a term for the numerous activities connected with the campaign. She lumped them all together and called them *politicking*. Politicking became a Spickard catchword.

Politicking for me began on that already eventful day, the twenty-eighth of March 1936, the day the *Gazette* acquired a godfather. A good-size crowd had gathered in the circuit courtroom in Trenton when I arrived and found a seat beside Maude Dean, Franklin township committeewoman. Maude was chief operator of the telephone exchange at Spickard and a good person to be near if you weren't acquainted with many people. She knew everyone at Spickard and a goodly number throughout the county. Telephone numbers were superfluous when Maude was at the switchboard. All you needed to do was take down the receiver and say, "*Gazette* office," or "Mrs. T. S. Wilson," or even "Ring Mother" or "Aunt Sadie." Maude did the rest. If the

MRS. SIMMONS IS CANDIDATE

Missouri Republican women should be particularly interested in the election this year for Mrs. George B. Simmons of Marshall, Missouri, is candidate for Congress from her district. Mrs. Simmons attained national prominence during the first Roosevelt administration by her articles on the farm situation, some of which appeared in the Saturday Evening Post. She has since been in demand as a speaker and because of a happy faculty for hitting the nail on the head and an overwhelming sincerity of purose she invariably gives her audience something worthwhile

Looking Forward
By Franklyn Waltman
Publicity Director, Republican National Committee

"Quick. Wallace! The hypodermic needle—before the election!"

Perhaps President Roosevelt did not use those exact words but they undoubtedly represent the substance of the instructions given to Secretary of Agriculture Wallace when the cries and groans of the suffering American farmers reached Washington. Of course, Mr. Roosevelt must have been surprised when he learned that prices of major farm products were lower than in 1933, for he repeatedly had told the farmers that everything was all right because "we are planning it that way — don't let anybody tell you differently.

Republican

Monday, October 17 — D
Tuesday, October 18 -
    Washington Twp.
Wednesday, October 1
    Liberty Twp.
Thursday, October 20
Friday, October 21 —
    Caulfield, Circuit
    3:30 p. m.
Friday, October 21 -
    Twp.
Saturday, October 2
    Circuit Court r
Monday, October 2
    Lincoln Twp.
Tueslay, October 2
Thursday, Octobe
Friday, October

Gazette Endorses Spickard Man

It has been called to the Gazette's attention that some criticism has been circulated in reference to an editorial, "Matter of Record," published September 22 in support of P. G. Wild of Spickard, Republican candidate for re-election as Grundy county's representative.

The Gazette is proud to have an opportunity to endorse a Spickard man for this important office, especially since Mr. Wild has shown by his vote that he is not controlled by any political machine and that he has kept in mind at all times the welfare of the people of Grundy county.

The inference that Mr. Wild is opposed to old age pensions is so ridiculous that it does not deserve recognition. Mr. Wild's stand on old age assistance may be verified by consulting the House Journal for 1935 recording the proceedings of the 58th general assembly. On page 1073 is given the vote on Committee Substitute for Senate Bill No. 7, the bill providing for old age pensions. There were no dissenting votes; the bill was passed unanimously; and the record shows that Mr. Wild was present and voted "Yes."

his election to the legislad promised the any

Let's Keep the Record Straight

When I first asked the people to send me to Jefferson City to represent them I made them two promises, one to the old people that I would vote for Old Age Assistance, second that I would oppose all increases in taxation.

I have kept my promises with the people and should I be reelected every statement I make I will endeavor to keep to the best of my ability.

P. G. WILD
Spickard, Mo.

N
Wil
for

The wo
whose
ley,"
newspa
introduc
of read
they ha
the lar

person you were calling was not at home, Maude knew at which neighbor's house to find her. She was a wonderful source of vital statistics. She knew whether the Browns had had their new baby yet or whether old Mr. Smith had lived through the night. Her assistant, Nina Clifton, a widow who supported three young sons on her meager salary, was just as efficient on the switchboard and always pleasant, although quiet and reticent.

The business of electing delegates to the party's district convention at Kirksville was disposed of quickly. There was a rather dry report by the resolutions committee, adopted without dissent, somewhat to my disgust, because delegates were going uninstructed and I thought everyone ought to go all-out for Alf Landon. Being new at politics, I knew nothing of not sticking your neck out. Being new in the county, I was not aware of the obligation Trenton folks felt to Arthur M. Hyde, former secretary of agriculture, or of his loyalty to Mr. Hoover, still a possibility, if a remote one.

The Republican county officers were introduced and spoke briefly, as did several candidates who had already announced. When they called on Jim Settles, editor of the *Galt Tribune,* and Bob Packwood of the *Republican-Times,* I had a hunch my turn was coming, so I decided what I would say. I related a little incident that happened on election day in 1932 when the chairman of the Democratic committee in the northern Kansas town where I had taught school was hauling voters to the polls. He stopped at the home of an elderly lady and offered to take her to vote.

"I'm going to tell you the truth," she admitted as she put on her coat. "I'm a Republican. I'm going to vote for Roosevelt, though. If he makes as good a president as his daddy did, he'll be a mighty fine president."

I concluded by offering my help and that of the *Gazette* to the end that no such mistake as to who the candidates and their parties were would be made in the coming battle and was generously applauded. After the meeting I met a number of people, including Jack Hoover, who invited me up to his law office and told me he was planning to run for prosecuting attorney and would stop at the *Gazette* office soon for an announcement and some candidate cards.

A political campaign is a wonderful break for a small, struggling newspaper. Announcements came in thick and fast during the next two months. The standard fee for one was five dollars, for which the name of the candidate and the office for which he was running appeared under his party heading each week until the primary in August. The successful candidates were continued on until the general election. We always ran a little news story about each one from whom we received a paid announcement. We kept the stories factual and were careful not to commit ourselves for any individual, although naturally we had our favorites. This impartiality was necessary if we were to be in a position to support the party's choice in the general election.

The office of sheriff seemed to be most attractive during that depression year. Six men had already announced for it when Bill Chrisman, a big, ungainly farmer from the southern part of the county, stopped me in front of the *Gazette* office one warm May afternoon and told me he was getting into the race.

Gwen had gone home for a few days' visit and I had just finished up her ad beat. We were going to have a good week, and five dollars more would make it super— the kind of week that lets you save something for an icy day—but Chrisman was hesitating about spending the five. Positive he didn't have a chance with so many other candidates in the field, including several with experience in running for office, I gave him a sales talk about how the Spickard people would appreciate seeing his name in their paper and the strength of the party in our territory and how the announcement would pave the way for him when he began house-to-house campaigning.

My conscience hurt almost as badly as my feet did from walking all over the business district selling advertising as I accepted his five dollars and his promise for a share of his candidate cards. Dan McKinnon and Ed Spickard were considered by far the strongest candidates, and I didn't see how this slow-talking farmer had a chance.

But fate takes strange turns. True, McKinnon was nominated and elected. But he made Bill Chrisman his deputy, and the next four years served to trim all the awkwardness from the quiet farmer. People liked him, and he made a host of friends. Missouri law at that time forbade a sheriff to succeed himself. Chrisman, with his four years of experience as a deputy, was a logical successor. He ran in 1940, was elected easily, and served a full four-year term. I've always been glad his five dollars was not thrown away.

"With a conscience like yours," Gwen would sometimes say, "its a wonder we ever make any money. I'm completely mercenary."

But it was she who slipped a subscription on the list for a shut-in who enjoyed every word of news about her lifelong acquaintances and whose old-age pension could not be stretched to include the price of the paper. Gwen was about as mercenary as a marshmallow.

Chapter 11

The People We Met

Gwen

In our family we had always described anyone a little
unusual as a "character" long before the expression
became universal slang. It was derived from a longer
expression, "a character in a book." After living in Spickard a couple of years, we decided characters in books
couldn't possibly be as unique and as interesting as the
people we met there. Never had we seen a place with so
many kinds of people, many with their own individual,
fascinating, real-life dramas, others with a personality
never duplicated on any movie set. The soap operas have
always been tame in comparison with the stories from
life we unearthed, accidentally and in the line of duty,
while we were on the *Gazette*.

Not that most of the citizens of Spickard weren't wonderful and weren't good to us. We had our ups and
downs and probably our enemies, but on the whole we
were treated fine—sometimes with a mixture of amusement at our venture, astonishment at our nerve, and

occasionally chagrin at our methods, but eventually with some respect, too, in an offhand way, at what we were trying to do and at the degree of success we were attaining.

The weekend after our first publication, I went down to the office to write letters home on the typewriter. I was suddenly aware that someone was staring at me, and I raised my head to stare right back at a quite astonishing lady standing in the doorway. She was decidedly stout, her face was a mass of lines that I confusedly kept trying to sort out into features (I can't to this day recall just what she looked like, although I saw her many times later), and her hair was an amazing shade of henna and, to put it kindly, windblown—an understatement if I ever made one. In fact it was wildly windblown.

I gulped. "Hello," I said weakly, wondering if by any chance she was as dangerous as she looked to me at the moment.

"Are either of you girls married?" she asked, her squinty little eyes darting over me until I felt positively undressed.

"No, we're not," I said as pleasantly as I could manage over my embarrassment and astonishment.

"Ever been married?" she barked.

"No," I answered.

"Gonna get married?" was the next thrust.

"Why, I suppose some day," was my brilliant reply. "I really don't know. I mean I haven't picked out anyone, I mean we neither of us has decided for sure . . ." I broke off, knowing I wasn't making sense to anyone, even myself. In fact, I was babbling.

"Well, I've been married three times," she asserted matter-of-factly but with an air of pride. "I know how to get 'em and I know how to get rid of 'em."

But before I could get any advice from the experienced, she whirled around and, for one of her bulk, padded off up the street at a surprising speed. Later I learned she definitely did know how to get them and how to get rid of them. She had had as many common-law husbands as legal ones, but in spite of her rather casual marital status she had also been one of the finest seamstresses in the county with a real talent for her trade, and she was generosity itself in her more prosperous days.

Another time Ardis and I both were too taken aback to have good sense. We had ordered a shipment of paper stock with the *Republican-Times* at Trenton in order to obtain a better quantity discount and save a little on shipping charges. They phoned that it was there and to send a truck for it. Ardis called a local garage and was assured the paper would be delivered in a couple of hours.

Some time later a two-ton truck drove up and unloaded, not the ton of paper we expected, but one small bundle weighing perhaps fifty pounds. The driver, however, was what took us off our feet. A tiny, wizened man crawled out from behind the wheel and demanded in a high, squeaky voice, "Where do you want this paper put?" Obviously he was so disgusted at the antics of a couple of fool girls who would send a truck for that amount of paper he could hardly contain himself. As for us, we were both so chagrined at the mix-up and so busy wondering how on earth that gnomelike figure could possibly heave those big bundles of paper into the high truck bed, we just stared.

"Was this what you wanted?" he repeated impatiently. "Where shall I put it?"

Ardis came to. "Is that all you've got?" she demanded

in her best withering schoolmarm manner. "You surely made some mistake—or someone did. There ought to be a lot more than that."

"That's all there is," he insisted stubbornly. For a minute I wondered who would win—my small determined sister or that small determined man.

"Bring the paper in here," I directed the man, just to jump into the breach as I always did when I sensed my sister clashing with someone. "You'd better run down to Trenton, Ardis, and conduct a search for the rest of the paper. Yes, thanks, put it right there," I told the man. "By the way, what is your name?"

Someone around the office spoke up hastily.

"You know Peahack, don't you?"

Peahack! The name fit like a bathing suit.

"Oh, yes, yes, of course," I assured them all. As though I could ever forget the face, the figure, or the name if I had ever encountered them before. But evidently it pleased him to think I could have forgotten, for he always spoke to me from then on with the greatest of friendliness, which I seldom saw him use on anyone else. Ardis did locate the missing paper, which had been stored in the *Republican-Times* warehouse, and all was straightened out, with Peahack delivering the paper the next day and proving to us he was stronger than he looked.

There was Mrs. T. S. Wilson, whose dignity and graciousness invariably made me feel she was Spickard society, each with a capital *S.* She really was a lovely person, and her manner was the type you associated with money and position, although in a small town you couldn't be well liked and still be a snob. And she was well liked. Maybe sometimes a jealous few might smile behind her back, but she commanded respect. I was a little awed by her until I found out how genuinely friendly she really was. In knowing her I learned how grateful a newspaper reporter is to anyone who will take the trouble to call with news of the club meetings, dinners, and gatherings that are the gist of a country newspaper. Her husband had made his original fortune by buying chickens and shipping them to the East.

I found, too, rather to my naive surprise, that grief is not assuaged by money. When I interviewed the banker's sister after his sudden death, her grief at her loss and at being the only one of the family left was as deep and heartrending as that of anyone else. It was rather a jolt to me to find out money could buy so few things. I don't know why I had always supposed people with a lot of money were invulnerable to any disaster, but I was gratified to have had that silly idea jarred out of me before it took hold and did some real damage.

There were dozens of other people who touched our lives in one way and another. We learned what poverty and want can do to men and women. We learned some of the reasons homes are broken. As a reporter I found myself looking with an impersonal eye at both sides of a dispute, analyzing the blame on both sides, seeing clearly the little foibles and weaknesses of people that cause trouble to themselves. As a person I felt warm sympathy and cold disdain, sometimes helpless anger, and occasionally a buoyant happiness at the things that happened to the people I was getting to know so well. I had to train myself rigidly to let no note of personal opinion creep into a news story while still keeping it human.

There was one person I met who definitely was a character. For the Christmas of 1935, I obtained some catalogs of Christmas cards that could be personalized and sold several orders. One day Edra said, "There is a nightclub in Trenton and I know the woman who runs it. I've done her hair. She wants some personalized cards and I told her I'd bring you in so she could see ours. It's a hard place to find."

"Fine!" I said, delighted at the prospect. "Thanks."

We twisted around a couple of crooked streets until I was completely confused, having a poor sense of direction anyway, and stopped in front of a large Victorian house set well back and somewhat obscured by large trees. It occurred to me it was a strange setting for a nightclub, but I was so busy balancing the big catalogs, my purse, the order book, and other things that I didn't dwell on it. My experience with real nightclubs was limited, even though I had played violin in a little orchestra at dances a few times.

Edra rang the bell, and I was startled when a little shutter opened and an eye appeared. The shutter closed, and a large man swung the heavy door open. I assumed he was the bouncer.

"Sally is in her office," he said. He seemed to know who we were and why we were there.

He led us down a long hall flanked on both sides by doors. Languid-looking young women in satiny dresses lounged in some of the doorways. I began to get the creeps. The man tapped on a door and opened it. Behind a desk was a middle-aged woman with heavy makeup and auburn sculptured curls.

"Oh, my gosh!" I thought, trying to freeze my face in an impersonal but businesslike expression. "This must be a madam."

Edra introduced me as "Miss Hamilton of the *Gazette* at Spickard" and her as "Sally."

"I have marked some pages of cards I thought you might consider," I said in my most professional manner, getting right down to business. I felt she was as eager for me to leave as I was to get out of there. She quickly chose the most un-Christmasy ones I had—pictures of cocktails surrounded by colored baubles. I was delighted with a $35.00 order, riches for that time. I filled out the order blank and collected half the amount as a deposit. She made no objection. Perhaps she was accustomed to cash in advance.

Back in the car I turned to Edra. "Don't you ever dare tell Ardis who this is for," I ordered her severely. She promised.

We delivered the cards later. When we got back to the shop, Kes looked at me with a strange expression on his face—questioning? Apprehensive? I didn't know.

"What did you think of Sally?" he asked.

I thought for a moment. "I once heard of a book titled *A House Is Not a Home*!"

He grinned, looking relieved, I thought.

"Not necessarily," he agreed.

Until I wrote this story, Ardis never knew who that big order for which she was so grateful had come from. It was just as well.

As the days rolled by, almost everyone brought to our notice some problem. Often these were solved, before or after we wrote stories about them, and sometimes because of the stories we wrote; sometimes they were never fully solved, but the people were all characters in the book of our first years on the *Gazette*, and from that panorama we were learning. Our appreciations were deepened, our senses sharpened, and our work became more and more fascinating. We were growing up.

And, of course, there was Orville, one of the first people I met when I came to Spickard. He was to become one of the most significant people I ever met.

Chapter 12

Printers I Have Known

Ardis

If the weather played a dominant note in the fluctuations of the *Gazette*'s prosperity, the printer-operator of the moment was a close second. A Linotype, usually referred to in a country print shop as "the machine," is a sensitive machine at its best, and our Model K definitely was not at its best by the time we became its proud owners. Our Linotype had a temperamental, unpredictable personality. We never really got on a friendly basis with it.

Like a small child, the machine would purr along angelically as long as its whims were humored; then on the slightest provocation or even for no apparent reason whatever it would behave in a most disturbing manner. Someone quipped that the person who invented the Linotype went crazy afterward and that all who had anything to do with one since that time often thought they would do likewise.

Owen, who followed Kes, was a slender dark-eyed lad

Dewey McDaniel was bitten in the shoulder last week by a cow which he was trying to drive from pasture. The cow attacked him several times and he was forced to strike her with a large club three times to protect himself. The cow, which was tied and was given camphor hydrophobia, recovered. Mr. McDaniel's wound was not serious.

Mrs. Margaret Bosley has rented her house east of town to Roy McLaughlin and family and has taken housekeeping rooms at the home of Mrs. Rhetta Gates.

Robert Bender of San Francisco is visiting his parents, Mr. and Mrs. O. H. Bender.

Mr. and Mrs. Walter Barnes and Mrs. Morton Thogmartin called on Mr. and Mrs. Otto Hamilon Sunday afternoon.

Mr. and Mrs. T. S. Wilson and Mr. and Mrs. O. B. Cowardin called on Mr. and Mrs. P. G. Wild Sunday evening.

O. C. Newton of Kansas City was a guest of Mr. and Mrs. Jay Ewing Sunday and Sunday evening.

Bryan Shriver of Kansas City spent the weekend with friends in this community.

Corvin Vincell of Los Angeles

* * * * * * * *
* UNCLE SAM'S *
* POCKETBOOK *
*   *
*   The official Daily Treasury *
* Statement on September 7 *
* showed the financial condi- *
* tion of the Treasury since July *
* 1 to be: *
* Expenditures .. $1,628,322,874.32 *
* Receipts .... $874,046,889.25 *
* In the hole .... $754,275,985.07 *
*   The gross Federal debt on *
* that date was $37,634,243,773.31, *
* Your per capita share of *
* that debt is $289.49. *
* * * * * * * *

— HURRY TO —

McCLURG SHOE HOSPITAL
And Save Your Sole and Get Well Heeled

Reasonable Guaranteed Service

2d Door West Graham's Grocery
E. 17th Street, Trenton, Mo.

MAN'S HEART STOPPED
    STOMACH GAS CAUSED
W. L. Adams was bloated so with gas that his heart often missed beats after eating. Adlerika rid him of all gas, and now he eats anything and feels fine.—D. G. Dennis, Druggist.

SPECIAL BARGAINS AT HARRY'S

Girsl' Sport Oxfords .... **$1.00**   Boys' Sturdy Built Shoes **$1.00**

Women's Arch Shoes **$1.69**   Men's Guar. Work Shoes **$1.49**

There's Shoes an' SHOES an' Then There's SHOES!

T R U E — Some are just mere foot coverings but they pass as Shoes at a CHEAP PRICE.

But if you really appreciate your feet, we invite you to try us for SHOES that are SHOES and Sold at Very Moderate Prices, too

Foster Shoe Store
Trenton   Missouri

JACK SPRAT Food STORES

Fri. and Sat.
SEPTEMBER 23d and 24th

Peaches Jack Sprat, Sliced or Halves, No. 2½ can **17c**

PEACHES, Jack Sprat, sliced or halves . 6 cans 99c
COFFEE, Jack Sprat .... 2 lb. cannister 49c

BANANAS, Golden ripe .... 4 lbs. 25c
ORANGES, Rich, juicy 288's .... 2 dozen 35c
HEAD LETTUCE, extra fancy .... 2 for 15c

SUGAR CORN, Mayflower, No. 2 can ... 3 cans 25c
SWEET PEAS, Mayflower, No. 2 can ... 3 cans 25c
SPINACH, Mayflower, No. 2 can ...... 3 cans 25c
HOMINY, Jack Sprat, No. 2½ can ..... 3 cans 25c

PINEAPPLE, Jack Sprat .... 3 8-oz. cans 25c
SUGAR, with $1.50 grocery order .. 10 lb. bag 49c
P & G SOAP, White Naptha .... 5 bars 19c
MATCHES, Blue Star .... 3 boxes 10c
PANCAKE FLOUR, Jack Sprat .... 3 lb. bag 15c

Oats Jack Sprat, Quick cooking, 3 lb. pkg. **16c**

SYRUP, Jack Sprat, Light .... No. 10 can 62c

Syrup Jack Sprat Dark, No. 10 can **16c**

LARD .... per lb. 11c

Drygoods **Bevan'S** Hardware
Groceries.

as beautiful as Adonis and just about as useful. He couldn't lift the page form to the cylinder press unless Gwen was around to balance one end for him. I wasn't any help because he was too much taller than I was. The only son in a family of older sisters, he was pleasant to get along with but had little sense of responsibility. He dated Shilah, a brown-eyed blonde who worked at Wilson's Grocery—that is, when he didn't stand her up. He had been known to go to sleep and forget he had a date. In that case he would take her to lunch the next day, usually at Hank's Cafe, and all would be forgiven.

Shortly after we printed the primary election ballots for the 1936 campaign—a job requiring thirty-six hours of solid work for me, with Owen and another boy alternating in shifts (I stopped only for coffee and sandwiches during the entire time), Shilah's older sister, Juanita, went to California to get her man. Soon the whole family followed and took Shilah with them, whereupon Owen decided he didn't want to be a printer-operator after all. He went to California, too, and got a job in a filling station.

His departure was without warning, but Howard Wilson of Princeton, who worked on the *Telegraph,* came down at night, set the type, and got the paper printed for three weeks. In the meantime the *Galt Tribune,* a hand-set weekly, folded and sold its subscription list to the *Trenton Republican-Times* and its equipment piecemeal. On the off chance that he might be interested, we offered the job to the former editor, Jim Settles, and to our surprise he took it, since it meant an opportunity to regain his speed on the Linotype. Settles moved his wife and three small sons to Spickard, and peace reigned in the print shop once more. In fact, peace was so sweet and he so steady that we just didn't take it seriously when he hinted we should be looking around for someone else, although we knew that because of his family responsibilities he could not continue indefinitely on the salary we could pay and that, like us, he was a frustrated writer, and with us he had no opportunity to write.

Finally, the blow came. Settles left for a better job, and Linwood Rogers came in answer to our advertisement. Linwood was good-hearted, but there were times when the Model K and he were not even on speaking terms. He had a talent for getting himself covered with ink. He slaughtered machinery. He possessed no sense of time. Just when things were at their worst, his pretty wife, Lola Lee, would pop in with some domestic problem. Lola Lee was a curly-headed blonde who could play the piano like nobody's business, but she couldn't boil water without burning it. She had been reared in affluence.

"Linwood," she would plead at four o'clock on press day when we were already an hour behind schedule, "What'll we have for dinner?"

"I don't know. You decide," Linwood would answer while I tried to keep my disgust hidden.

Although we were paying Linwood more than we had paid anyone before, they were always broke, in spite of the fact that her grandmother, whom they called "Mommy," frequently helped them out.

"We could have ice cream, but it's terribly expensive," Lola Lee would suggest.

"You know I like ice cream, but we'd better make it easy on Mommy," Linwood would say. Usually they had ice cream.

In the meantime I had been working on the machine in my spare time, and in a few months I got so I could set a fair string of type with exceptionally clean proofs. The keyboard was easy for me, but I hadn't the slightest conception of the mechanism and was completely helpless if anything went wrong. I hated selling advertising, though, and I hoped eventually I could set type and hire a man who could do the printing, service the machine, and help out with the ads. He would not need to know the keyboard if he was mechanical enough to keep the machine clean and functioning.

Alas for fond dreams. When Linwood left we hired a young man from Liberty who had some experience as a printer in the college there and said he could sell advertising. We had bank statements to publish that week, and I got along with them all right, although the composition was somewhat tedious and it was a standing joke that whenever we had anyone new on the machine it was always bank-statement time. Then on Tuesday, Pete Taylor from Taylor's department store and grocery brought in a complicated two-page ad requiring a great deal of makeup as well as typesetting, and since two-page ads don't grow on trees we couldn't say a thing.

At this time our usual schedule was to print on Thursday afternoons. The people in Spickard got their paper that evening if they went to the post office for it, and those on the rural routes received theirs Friday morning. That allowed some leeway, since if anything went wrong we could work late and still make the rural delivery.

This time we were ready to go to press at midnight when a severe electrical storm came up and the power went off. Gwen folded up at her desk, and the printer lay down on a stack of newsprint and went to sleep. I kept watch until the current was restored. I woke everyone up. There was just enough time if nothing else happened. The sun was coming up when I dragged the heavy mailbag across the street to the post office where the rural carriers were getting ready to sort up the mail. I sent the *Gazette* force home to catch up on sleep. Disliking to go to bed more than almost anything else, I always kept the shop open after those occasional all-night stretches, but I insisted the rest should take the day off.

The printer, in addition to knowing nothing about the machine, had a strong affinity for a beer parlor at the end of the block. Later in the week, after he had spent the greater part of the morning there, I fired him and he quit all at the same time. I have never known who beat the other to the draw.

For the next two months we didn't know from one issue to the next who was going to get the paper out. Part of the time I set the type and part of the time the current operator did. Gwen became quite proficient at setting headlines and ads by hand, and I learned to make up the front page, although I could never get the heads quite tight enough and someone usually had to go over them and tighten them up while I hovered anxiously hoping when the form was lifted the whole thing wouldn't collapse on the floor and have to be redone. It never did.

We had some characters who were laughable, some who were pathetic. There was one fellow who professed to have experience, but it turned out he handled printing machinery as though he were a blacksmith, not a printer. Working on the cement floor hurt his feet, so he calmly took off his shoes and socks and continued to go barefoot while I alternately hoped he would step on a hot slug and prayed that none of my political friends or good advertisers would drop in until we got the paper out. Then he, too, quit.

We received a postcard a few days later. "Dear Miss Hamilton," he had scrawled, "please look in a box and send me my insurance." Someone had sold him an insurance policy during the week. He had been forever putting things away in a box—any box that happened to be handy—and forgetting where they were. He had also neglected to tell us he had traded our advertising for his premiums.

Finally we advertised again and almost ended up with two operators on our hands. First, a man from Kansas City answered our ad; although we weren't too pleased with his letter, we decided to give him a try. Then it looked as though he was not coming, so we accepted an applicant from Pittsburg, Kansas. The two men met on the train en route to Trenton, became acquainted, and shared a cab to Spickard.

How to select one of these new applicants and get rid of the other was quite a problem. I hurried home and got Gwen and we had a round-table interview. The Kansas City man obviously didn't want the job, but he was out the expenses for his trip. The Pittsburg man wanted it but felt the other should not have to forgo his expense money, so I paid the former his train fare and S. F. Tavernaro, henceforth to be known as Tavvy, went to work for us.

Tavvy was small and dark, the son of Italian immigrants, although he was an American by birth and educated in the Pittsburg schools, where he had learned his trade. He mastered the idiosyncrasies of the Model K, and from then on I had no more worries with it except for buying an occasional part, due to normal wear and tear. He was exceedingly neat. He wore long-sleeve shirts all the time, and I never saw him with ink on his clothes. Once in a while when the machine was behaving badly or the autocaster, which converted metal into cuts, refused to cast, I would hear him swearing in his soft Latin voice, but he was quiet and reserved. He wasted coal and wood and had a habit of building up the fire just before quitting time, to the distress of all my Scottish ancestry, but he got the paper out on time, he made it look nice, and he took good care of the machinery.

Sometimes he grew restless. I always told him if he could better himself to go ahead and I would give him a good recommendation, that all I asked was two weeks' notice. He wasn't making much money, but his expenses were so low he could actually save more in Spickard than in many other places at twice the salary. Room and board were six dollars a week; laundry was fifty cents. I tried to make it up to him in other ways, too. If he wanted to visit his brother in Kansas City on weekends or holidays, his time was his own as long as he got the paper out. He could leave Thursday evening and stay away until Tuesday if he liked, provided he met the usual Thursday deadline. A few extra hours' work on Wednesday night might be necessary, but that was up to him. It was results, not the number of hours, that counted.

We got along well together, but I never felt really well acquainted. Even Gwen, who complained she seldom went into a café for a sandwich without someone on the next stool telling her the story of his or her life, didn't break his reserve for nearly two years. After we sold the *Gazette* he confided to Gwen that he wished I would buy another paper; he would like to work for me again. I considered that one of the nicest compliments I ever had and was planning to do just that when World War II came along and Uncle Sam claimed him. I heard he came through the war safely, and although our paths have gone in different directions, I never think of him without a wish that things have gone well for him and that he is happy.

We really slaved to keep the standards of the paper high, mechanically as well as otherwise. If we seem to brag a bit over the way it was received—maybe we were a little cocky—it was in part because we received so many good comments and so little real criticism. Of course the hot Democrats thought we were too Republican and the hot Republicans thought we were not Republican enough—Gwen did her best to keep the paper as nonpartisan as possible—but that was to be expected.

Chapter 13

Personals

Gwen

With Ardis it was always the paper. With me it was always the people, which was the reason, I suppose, that I found it fun to walk up and down Main Street, stopping at each place of business from lumberyard to pool hall to ask people about where they had been, who had visited them, and other little items that made up not only their lives but the personals column that was sometimes the first thing the readers looked for.

If, as our family saying went, people who were unique were "characters out of a book," Spickard had a bookcase full. More than half a century later many of these characters are still unforgettable, but just a few stories will illustrate what it was like in Spickard in the late 1930s. I suppose Spickard was more or less typical of small towns everywhere, but we had fallen in love with it, so we saw it through different lenses.

In such a small place everybody knew everybody else; therefore no scandal, no divorce, no affairs, no illegiti-

CLASSIFIED

Quick

SERVICE

WANTED TO TRADE: wood or kindling for subscriptions. Will also trade for anything else we can use. The Gazette.

FOR SALE: 2 piece living room suite; 4 piece walnut bedroom suite; good piano. Kitchen cab-

around
spickard

C. E. Schooler made a business trip to Quincy Wednesday. Mrs. Schooler, R. B. Nichols and Joe Kincade accompanied him.

Mr. and Mrs. Otto Hamilton and Mrs. J. S. Wiggins were Sunday guests of L. M. Barnes and family of Tindall.

Mr. and Mrs. Vernon Brown and Mrs. Ellen Brown spent Sunday at Half Rock and Trenton.

Mr. and Mrs. George Ledford and Miss Lena Keith and Miss Bonnie Wild attended the bankers' convention and an evening banquet at Chillicothe Friday.

Miss Edra Gose spent the weekend with her parents, Mr. and Mrs. D. G. Gose.

R. H. Newton returned Tuesday to his home in Kansas City after a visit with Mr. and Mrs. Jay Ewing.

Kathryn J. Logan was a weekend guest of Miss Alma Lundy of Trenton.

Mr. and Mrs. Ernest Cooper

inets. Several good German heaters. Sweigart's Furniture Home, 918 Main, Trenton, Mo.

200 acre stock and grain farm, 4 miles from Mill Grove on rock road. 7 room house, 3 good barns and other outbuildings. Priced for quick sale. R. W. Crane, Trenton, Mo., Phone 354.

FOR SALE: 2 burner electric hot Plate almost new. Inquire at the Gazette.

———o———

Churches

UNITED BRETHREN REVIVAL

Revival at the Spickard United Brethren church will begin Sunday, November 13. Sunday school at 10:00 a. m. and preaching 11:00 a. m. and 7:30 p. m.

Song services begins each evening at 7:30 as long as the meeting lasts, two or three weeks. This revival is for the good of the town and community so we invite everybody to come and have part in doing good.

The old time gospel that grips the soul and makes people want to be and do better will be preached. Come.

W. M. Pettibon, pastor.

Mrs. Margaret Bosley went to Trenton Monday for several days' visit with her daughter, Mrs. Roy Reams and family.

Dr. and Mrs. W. T. Pittman visited at the C. T. Perry home Saturday afternoon.

Mr. and Mrs. Fred Walkenhorst of Kansas City were weekend guests of her parents, Mr. and Mrs. C. B. Cook.

Mr. and Mrs. Vernon Brown and family were guests of her parents at Melbourne, Sunday, October 2. While there they watched the construction of a pond an acre and a half in size by means of a caterpillar tractor and a scraper.

mate birth was ever a secret for very long, and sometimes it seemed everyone but the participant knew what
was going on. Yet I seldom heard vicious gossip. Not
only did everyone know everyone else, but an amazing
number were related to each other. I learned very quickly
never to make the slightest disparaging remark about
anyone; I was probably talking to his or her cousin or
best friend.

Not that the cousin would have cared too much—
there was a surprising amount of tolerance, considering
that this was the late 1930s and all the so-called free-
doms of the 1990s were unheard-of. There was also a
considerable mix of educated and illiterate, affluent
and poor, leaders and followers, or just hangers-on. Occasionally there was an eruption of some kind, usually
caused by jealousy and alcohol, or one born of despair—
these were the depression days—but there was an abundance of goodwill and helpfulness, too. Many of the
residents were third- and fourth-generation Grundy
Countians.

As the new kids in town, we were viewed at first with
curiosity and skepticism mixed with caution, but as we
romped into local interests, attended churches, and reported on school activities, political doings, or whatever
else came along, we began to receive comfortable acceptance. The cutting edge, of course, was the paper.
People loved reading their own and their neighbors'
names, even though they might know all about the event
before it came out in weekly print. They never told me
in journalism school that the secret of success was
getting lots of names in the paper. Come to think of it,
they never told me much of anything about a country
weekly.

Success meant selling enough subscriptions that the

local merchants would feel buying advertising was a profitable thing. Therefore, we came to be big promoters of the Summer Saturday Night programs sponsored by the merchants of Spickard and added a few free subscriptions to the other items in the collection gathered up each week for the "drawing." People registered on tickets they received with purchases and threw their names into a barrel; then at the end of the program someone drew names for the prizes. Sometimes a money prize was the big attraction, especially if the fund had built up by being carried over when the person whose name was drawn the previous week was not present.

An outdoor stage was set up and cash prizes were given for winning amateur performances, judged by a panel instructed to watch the audience reaction in making selections. Then the town of five or six hundred became a teeming metropolis of at least two thousand on a nice Saturday night. People came from a radius of more than thirty miles on horseback, in wagons, or on foot. The automobiles jammed all of the streets. In spite of the depression, business boomed on Saturday nights.

I would watch the program, perform whatever duties it seemed befitting for an editor to do, and then, as the crowd broke up, scamper up to the drugstore and pick up a couple of bucks scooping ice cream for the crowd. Ice cream cones were five cents each, as were cokes and hamburgers, so for less than fifty cents a fellow could buy a couple of gallons of gas at nineteen cents per gallon, drive into Spickard, and treat his girl to entertainment and a soda. For less than a dollar—if he had a dollar—he could take her to the café and buy a hamburger, soda, and pie for both of them. A quarter would buy a whole meal for one person. The guys who could afford that were pretty popular as a rule.

Charlie Schooler was one of the movers and shakers who got the Saturday night programs going. He owned Schooler's Furniture Store and a funeral home in Spickard, had been mayor, and was in on everything the town did—and since he had most of the money, they jolly well better do it his way. He was also something of a ham— he had led a Boy Scout band and toted them around the state some years before. I am not sure he had musical training, but since the band members had all grown up by the time we lived there and I never heard them play, who am I to judge? Kids who might never have had the opportunity to get out of Grundy County saw at least a bit of the world in northwest Missouri.

Anyway, Charlie booked the Saturday night acts, emceed the programs, and saw to it things moved. I remember I was supposed to be around on Saturday nights, and it seems that I had a title of secretary or something, but whatever it was, I was there because these events were good for business, because they were always good for a feature story or two, and because I was about as big a ham as Charlie. I sometimes played the piano for someone to give a vocal or instrumental solo, and I was just as much of an amateur as the rest. I was disqualified from competition, of course, since, being connected with the paper, I was one of the promoters.

I remember that the Wilburn sisters, who sang country songs with a real country twang, entered often and sometimes won. Their mother, whom we always addressed as Mrs. Wilburn, was one of our best country correspondents—a person who sent in news from her school district each week in exchange for a subscription to the paper. Mrs. Wilburn wrote a beautiful hand and used correct grammar. She always, it seemed, had a baby in her arms, a red-headed toddler clinging to her skirt, and small fry stair-stepped up to teenagers, in a quantity I never discerned. All were shiny clean and neatly dressed, even though their clothes might be a bit faded, patched, or handed down. Sometimes Mr. Wilburn, obviously proud of his brood, especially the performers, carried a child or two, but I seldom saw him. I knew he must be around, though—all those children. I wonder what happened to them all.

Warm weeknights were fun, too. One evening a week the stores stayed open late, and the group of young people who had voted for president for the first time in the 1936 election would gather on the steps of the furniture store and enjoy the passing parade.

There was Ross Wise, Charlie's protégé. Fatherless, Ross had started at the age of about ten or twelve to work for Charlie, who was childless. Their relationship always appeared friendly but not especially warm. Ross got along well with everyone, was low-key, and put up with inconveniences like being on call twenty-four hours a day, seven days a week, with a tolerance few would have displayed. Eventually, he inherited the furniture store and funeral home, but he had earned them many times over in low pay, hours spent, and loyalty.

Son, Jo-Dad, Brandy, and Coot, the Kirk brothers, lived out in the hills and came to town on the first of the month to cash their mother's Civil War widow's pension check and buy their few supplies. The rest of the money became liquefied—or liquor-fied—fairly quickly. One night one of them ran out of money before the liquor store closed and touched Ross for a loan. Ross good-naturedly explained he didn't have any money so he couldn't lend any. The Kirks were illiterate but not necessarily dumb. This brother (I never did learn which was which) tried all sorts of persuasion and got repeated refusals. Finally, he played his trump card. He squared off in front of Ross, hands in overall pockets, eyes a bit bleary, and, waving slightly, intoned, "All right for you, Ross Wise. My old mother, she's ninety-six years old, and we'll just go to Noel Moss." Moss was the undertaker at Princeton, twelve miles to the north. Ross remained unmoved.

On the steps with me by that time was Orville, who had also worked for Charlie Schooler during his high school years. Ross's wife, Nathelin, dark eyes sparkling, was always good for a fast quip. John Earl Keith, who had the talent and the desire to be a professional base-ball player until a knee injury robbed him of the knee joint and his opportunity, came up after he had closed the service station he and the bank owned and he oper-ated. With him was Lucille, his girlfriend, later his wife. John Earl pitched for the Spickard baseball team, knee notwithstanding, and the talk was often of a Sunday game, past or future. We made our own entertainment in those days, and Lucille, Nathelin, and I cheered the players on with gusto in spite of heat, chiggers, mosqui-toes, and other annoyances. John Earl and Orville, who had a mail-order print shop, were but two of the young entrepreneurs who found it easier and more profitable to create a job than to find one elsewhere.

Bevan's Grocery Store, in addition to weekly ads, sup-plied Spickard with seven attractive girls, daughters of the owner and his wife. Several of the older ones worked regularly in the store. Pretty dark-haired Genevieve, called Gen, was near my age, and we became friendly. Loren Brokaw thought she was pretty, too. They have cele-brated their golden wedding anniversary, and I still see them when they travel from their home in Arizona to visit relatives in Missouri and Iowa.

Passing by the group on the steps might have been P. G. Wild, state representative and Republican party leader in the county—another mover and shaker. He was one of those responsible for getting the canning factory in Spickard, where tomatoes and green beans grew well and where the government was willing to subsidize some jobs by aiding with the financing. After the season for vegetables was over, P. G. and some others pulled off a coup and obtained an orchard of pears to can.

One of the products was pear cider and, expecting a story on the success of the pear venture, P. G. brought a gallon over to the newspaper office. The fall day was warm, the cider cold, and since I did not especially care for it, I drank only a little, leaving plenty for Kes and Ardis, both of whom thought it was delicious. By the middle of the afternoon, I became aware that both were making frequent stops in their work and disappearing, he toward the pool hall, she toward home. Knowing the shortage of restrooms on Main Street and Ardis's loathing of public facilities, it didn't take me long to figure out that pear cider had unadvertised properties—at least unadvertised in print. Their behavior would have given any observing person a clue. I felt sorry for them, but it took great restraint on my part to keep from giving them a rougher time than they were already having.

P. G. saw to it that my very Republican sister received introductions at all the Republican meetings, which meant, of course, that the Republicans got publicity in the *Grundy County Gazette*. I don't know whether P. G. went home to bed in sorrow when Landon lost to Roosevelt in 1936, but Ardis did.

There was Old Doc McClanahan (as distinguished from young Doc, his son, who had a thriving practice in

Kansas City), who made daytime and nighttime house calls appreciated by almost everyone. It was his lovely wife who won everyone's affection and admiration. Not only did she put up with Doc's eccentricities and bouts with alcohol with grace and at least outward serenity, but she also retained her intelligence, her interest in everything, and her charm after her complete loss of vision. The couple who took care of her household and drove for Doc were in her trust, even though the man had served time in prison. I always suspected her attitude of tolerance spread over the town more than many people realized. She was greatly respected.

Kenny Fox, a handsome young man who was a victim of polio that had made walking difficult, sometimes joined us on the steps. He had a professional-quality tenor voice, and we spent hours harmonizing, the group of us. We were saddened and sobered when he lost his life in an accident—and with him that talent was gone. We were learning—not only about newspapers but also about life.

There were a number of churches in Spickard. I attended the Methodist, which was the one I had grown up in, and sometimes sang in the choir. The minister was really a better carpenter than preacher and had to supplement his rather spotty income from his congregation by carpentering. He was kind and generous, a quiet man who raised wonderful gardens and shared his crops with his neighbors, including us. That was one of the unexpected bonuses when we moved into our second house, across the street from them. His wife was a waif of a woman who played piano beautifully and often was so energetic that she completely wore out her frail body and lapsed into inertia for a time. They had a lovely teenage daughter, also talented musically. We enjoyed some sessions, the three of us, on Sunday afternoons.

The minister of the Christian church was not a resident of Spickard but lived in Princeton and served several area churches. He was especially good with young people, and I was drafted—willingly—to sing in special services he conducted. He was a trained musician and a fine person, I thought.

Then there was Sister Grace, pastor of a small church that might be considered a part of a cult now. Sometimes they were called Holy Rollers, but they were not the same as the group usually designated as such. Their small building was only a short distance away from our home, so we pretty much knew from the sounds what went on there at "meetin's." A few people spoke in tongues and there was much noise. Sister Grace's following was small but loyal; she led them with firmness and passion. Spickard never seemed to have any prejudice against a woman preacher, but when a breath of scandal, as far as I know never really proved, swept over her private life and money dealings, the atmosphere grew cool, and eventually she left town. Spickardites were tolerant, but they had their standards, especially for their preachers. Rather than confusing me, all these encounters with religion served to make me think, to examine and analyze; as a result, I believe I developed a stronger faith than I would have had without them.

There were many other interesting people—wise, funny, sad, pathetic, amusing, ambitious, worthless, philosophic, practical—and they became Spickard. I am sure I must have been exasperated or angry at them sometimes, but I don't remember it now. Looking back, I seem to be viewing an old watercolor, a bit faded, misty, with spots of light and shadow, bright and dark, but still clear enough for me to see the scene. And the scene still reveals what it was like to be young and poor and adventurous in an era that no longer exists. I'm grateful to have experienced that bit of Americana in the office of a little country newspaper, the *Grundy County Gazette.*

Chapter 14

Even a Romance

Gwen

This is a story of Ardis and me, mostly, in the days when our hearts were young and, if not always merry, at least quite our own. Still, romance is likely to invade at some time or another when two young girls start out on a venture. Ardis once tried to make me promise, before we bought the paper, that I wouldn't marry and leave her, but I wasn't having any.

The first time we saw Orville was that fateful day we bought the paper. There was a slender, very young-looking, black-haired fellow reading the exchanges, and presently I noticed he was gone. I promptly forgot him—that was the kind of impression he made on me.

When we took over the *Gazette* a couple of weeks later, the same young man appeared on the scene again. That time I noticed his eyes were a very dark blue and he was quite good-looking. I supposed he was about seventeen—and that ability of his to look far younger than he was bothered me for the next ten years.

Orville Thogmartin took this picture of Gwen Hamilton two months before they were married and says it is his favorite snapshot of her. Gwen says she was so proud of her new all-wool coat. It cost ten dollars!

---o---
BED NOTES

By Orville C. Thogmartin
THE BLACK WIDOW MURDER

On our back porch the other day we captured alive and singlehanded a deadly Black Widow Spider. The tiny red "hour glass" marking identifies him. Three flickers and he would have skittered out of sight, so swift were his lanky legs, had we not hastily urged him into a tiny box, which we then covered with cellophane and carried to a microscope. A huge, green, wicked fly pestering overhead was also shoved into the box, much against his will.

It is said a widow will jump at any chance. If we had had any doubts that this was a true widow, they vanished now. No, we didn't see him jump. But after blinking our eyes, we perceived what we thought was the Louis-Carnera fistic bout, only we think Louis is not so good a fighter as as this black spider, and also Carnera is not so good as this particular huge green, wicked fly.

Anyway, the spider was clinching and as a referee we separated them and the fly buzzed off. And with no further delay we dropped the Black Widow upon the floor and lightly but firmly stepped upon his neck. It was the first time we had ever deliberately committed murder, but we are a bachelor and all widows are deadly, we have heard, especially where bachelors are concerned.

And, Ohyes! we know again for certain that the spider was a Black Widow because we found the fly lying on the floor next morning— dead by poison. We know it was the same fly on account of he was so particularly huge and green and wicked.

* * * *

Legal Publications

ORDER (   )N

STATE (
County (
IN THI
vember
Ralph

Marth
  Nov
tiff h
J. H
and
otn
tha
of

Orville explained he was writing a column for free—
that he was working toward becoming a writer and wanted
experience. We offered to help him in any way we
could, although after I read a few of the columns I had
a notion to take back the offer—he was a far better
writer than I from the standpoint of careful thinking
and construction. He seldom wrote with dash and inspiration, but every word was judiciously chosen. The column included a number of things and varied from
week to week. There were usually paragraphs of impres-
sions of local scenes and happenings, humorous remarks,
sometimes a bit of poetry. The whimsical title, "Bed
Notes," intrigued me, and I discovered the column had
been started during a bout with rheumatic fever that
had begun about four years before and was not at that
time entirely routed. The effects from that battle Orville was to carry the rest of his life, and no one realized
it better than he, but he never mentioned it and sought
no sympathy or special consideration. What he could
do, he just did, quietly and thoroughly. He learned a
technique for saying "no" that served him the rest of
his life when it became necessary to use it.

For more than a year Orville drifted in and out of the
office, reading the exchanges, commenting occasionally on something we had done that he especially liked.
We learned that his opinion was never given lightly and
that he appreciated the improvements we were trying to
make more than most of our readers did. He had a keen
sense of humor, and as his health improved he appeared
more and more often in the shop and joined in the ban-
ter, sometimes with an apt remark that made me realize
suddenly, one day, that here was a person with strength of
character and a personality that grew on you somehow.
He never bothered to throw his personality around.

One day he dropped into the shop with his column and announced he was going to a dinner in honor of his birthday. Quite idly I asked, "How old are you?"

"Twenty-two," he said.

"You are?" I responded. "What a coincidence. I was twenty-two just six weeks ago."

"We're the same ages now, then," he grinned, and suddenly, irrelevantly, I noticed what an attractive smile he had. For a minute we stood smiling at each other companionably in a way old friends do. I thought, "Why haven't I paid more attention to Orville? He is quite the nicest of any of the boys in town." Afterward he told me he thought at the same moment he'd like to know me better.

A week or two later I was helping out at the drugstore after the Saturday night program (the size of the crowd strained the facilities of the one soda fountain to serve ice cream and sodas so badly that they had hired me as an extra for the rush hour). It was nearly midnight and I was frazzled. Orville drifted up, immaculate in white slacks and shirt, and I was feeling frowsy as all get out when he said, "Want a Coke?"

"Sure do," I answered, feelingly, and he grinned at me again. Suddenly I felt young and attractive and ready for anything.

Well, nothing happened. After we had our sodas I remarked, "Guess I'd better get home. It's late."

"I'll walk part way—I'm going home," Orville said. And when we reached the point where he went on up the hill and I went south to our house we said good night casually and went our ways. Once again I felt frazzled and frowsy as all get out.

But, just in case, I took a little extra special trouble with my dressing before I went to the drugstore the next

Saturday night. And this time he walked me home. I was glad even in the dark that I had carried a compact and lipstick in my purse and had taken time to use them before I started to work at about ten o'clock.

Maybe it wasn't coincidence he seemed to drop into the office more often than usual after that. Saturday night programs were soon over as fall approached, but he got in the habit of dropping in at the house sometimes, and we'd go to a church youth meeting together. His mother, Lera Thogmartin, he told me, had taught a class at the Christian Church there for many years, and he was much interested in church work. A couple of other nights he dropped in without making a date, so I proceeded to be gone a few times when I thought he might come. After that he made a date. I wasn't one to run a risk of being all ready and not having him come or not being ready and having him come. But I hoped he'd come.

But Orville had fallen in love—not with me, but with a printing press! For the work he was doing with his writing, he needed some stationery and other printed items, and he had also decided a small mail-order business would work in nicely with a writing career and was a quicker way, perhaps, of picking up a little lucre. In those depression days, you had to earn your spending money, if you had any, and jobs were as scarce as Republicans in Kansas in 1936.

When Orville found how expensive it was to buy printing—we did our best by him, but thrifty Ardis always had the payroll in mind and knew we had to pay the help and therefore we had to make a little profit—he decided to buy a little handpress and do his own printing. So he traded an old typewriter for a printing press and waded in. In one day's time he had decided here was his career, and shortly afterward he started specializing in gummed labels and stickers, selling by mail. He could print, write his own advertising, and have a mail-order business, all the things he wanted to do, in one package.

Having set his course, he was to let nothing except a global war ever deviate him from it. He learned printing as any self-educated person learns. He read every trade magazine he could get his hands on. He studied labels on drugstore bottles. He talked shop with printers in every town he had occasion to be in. He criticized and compared and lived printing. He continued that all his life. He'd rather be a poor printer than be rich at something else, and when asked his occupation he would put more pride in "I'm a printer" than he could have in "I'm president of the United States."

He had some success with his writing, too. He sold stories to boys' magazines and church publications and several pieces of poetry and articles to other papers. In addition, he had a number of things printed gratis in fairly high-class publications. But printing appealed to his very definite mechanical talent, satisfied his sense of the artistic and his creative ability, and seemed to have a quicker return as far as earning a living was concerned. With Orville, I'm sure that was the last consideration, however.

Thus, in addition to talking writing, we talked printing. He worked down at the shop quite often, learning more than we knew in nothing flat as far as operating any kind of machinery was concerned.

More and more often we found things we both liked to do. We didn't have any money for amusements, but we had fun. We loved to walk down to the river bridge and talk about all the deep subjects young people falling in love always discuss with such authority and agree-ability. I found if I didn't agree I had better keep still because he could always out-argue me, and if I wanted to go on thinking my way I had better not listen to him. There was no use in trying to convince him—he had a decided mind of his own. I don't remember what we discussed and what we said, and I'm glad I don't—our opinions then probably would only embarrass me now. But I do remember the sense of companionship I had and how content I was just to talk or sit silently, if that was what we felt like doing, and watch the river flow by. Sometimes we'd dream dreams of the places we would like to go and the things we'd like to do, but always a little wistfully, knowing somehow, with the wisdom of depression youth, that most dreams are seldom realized and the fun is in the dreaming.

Sometimes we would gather hickory nuts from the woods, and I would wonder a little at the trees and the denseness of the underbrush, which looked to my Kansas eyes like a jungle. Friends of ours were later to tell the joke of the Texas girl who came to north Missouri to visit in the spring when the lush green foliage of the woods and the pastures was at its richest. Her hostess asked her how she liked their country. "Ah, don't know yet, Mrs. Roberts," she said seriously. "Ah cawn't see it fo' the trees." That was good for a hilarious laugh in any crowd, but I always felt a little stab of sympathy for her. I knew what she meant, although her part of Texas was much drier than my part of Kansas.

One cold night in January, only about four months after Orville and I had mutually, without discussion, abandoned running around with almost anyone else, Orville told me he had that day realized he was in love with me. I was a little surprised. I had known for weeks I was in love with him, that he was the man I wanted to marry. I knew also, with a positiveness that surprised me, that I had never really been solely and exclusively a career girl at heart. I had liked the adventure, I had loved the writing, but what I wanted too in life was a real home of my own, where I could cook and putter if I liked, and watch my children grow up. I knew I would always like to take part in things and that I would help to earn the living if it seemed best, but a home would be a most important interest always. I was just made that way. People have always mattered more than anything, and a love for people—all sizes—for me finds fullest expression in homemaking.

I knew, too, that the man with whom I shared my life would have to have courage, high ideals, and a sense of humor and would have to like some of the things I liked, such as reading, public affairs, kids, and other people. My work on the *Gazette* had given me an awareness of what was important to me. I had also learned that couples did not always need to agree on everything. Orville felt the same way about many things, and although we did sometimes have our differences, as everyone does, I knew he was the man for me.

We were married the next October, a little more than a year after we had discovered we were the same age. All summer we had planned—or, now that I think of it, I had planned—that we would wait a few years until we had a little more money saved or he had his business built up. Orville, however, saw no reason for waiting. Through the years of struggle with the aftereffects of rheumatic fever and the adversity of the depression, he had learned to face the future with courage and confidence. He had won a battle for life. By comparison, nothing else was impossible.

Ardis hit the ceiling at first at the idea of my marrying a man with what she perceived as no prospects beyond a small business. After she had had time to absorb the idea she realized, however, that I had grown up, and she rallied round like the good sport she was. We made our plans to divide our household effects and split up housekeeping.

The shop work was routine by then, and since there was always the necessity of hiring one man, Ardis was fully capable of handling the *Gazette* by herself except during rush seasons. I would continue to write features, always my favorite job, and cover a story for her now and then if she wanted. She had never been greatly interested in the job-printing department other than as a profit-making part of the business, so we agreed that Orville would take it over. His study of printing had given him the ability to design and produce a superior product, and Ardis was happy to let us handle that work.

We realized it was better for us not to try to work together all of the time under the circumstances. When you get three such decided people as Ardis, Orville, and me in one small print shop, even the type might have to give sometimes, and as some of our printers sometimes reminded us, they don't make rubber type.

Besides, things were still more important to Ardis than people, especially if the thing was the *Gazette*. It was her baby. Before I left we had solved our help problem with reliable Tavvy, who could do all the mechanical work easily if he did not have to do the job printing, too. Fortunately, he was with her until she was ready to look for greener pastures.

Orville and I spent thirty years together—busy, sometimes tough, wonderful years before his death. We shared the fun of our printing business, two fine sons, and more happiness than we had a right to expect. We shared tragedy when we lost our younger son, Kerry, at age fourteen in an accident, but together we saw our older son, Clyde, graduate cum laude and earn his doctorate in Romance linguistics. I deeply regretted that his father was not living to share my pride in Clyde's success as a professor at a state university, and my happiness when he married Janis Gilbert, a beautiful and talented singer who has been an ideal daughter-in-law.

I have been blessed as well with my in-laws. Orville's mother, Lera, would take my part against Orville in almost any discussion, and of his father, Morton, Lera once remarked, "If Mort says anyone is ornery, they must be really bad." The rest of the family consisted of an older brother, Owen, who sought his fortune on the West Coast, and two sisters, pretty brown-eyed Helen, who worked as a bookkeeper at Pete Taylor's department store when we were in Spickard, and charming Frances, the youngest, whom everybody liked.

The Thogmartins, like so many of the families of the Spickard community, had been there for several generations, until the depression and war years took the younger generation, like so many others, away from their hometown to various parts of the country. That was a part of the picture of the 1930s.

Chapter 15

Lost and Found

Ardis

During the summer of 1937 we never were certain who our help would be by the time the next issue went to press. The series of inefficient operators meant frequent repairs to the machine, and between trying to set type at night to help out and worrying over expenses I had little time to think about anything else. In off moments I noticed Gwen and Orville were seeing more of each other and felt some concern lest they become serious, not dreaming that such a thing had occurred months before. It was not that I objected to Orville personally but that simply, from my point of view, becoming seriously interested in anyone with no money and only an infant business was unthinkable.

Gwen's announcement, late in the summer, that they were setting the date for October came as a complete shock to me, which was a surprise to her. I reminded her that she had once promised me at least six months' warning if she ever decided to marry and leave me, and she reminded me that she had never agreed to promise that.

Fortunately, there was too much to do to give me much time to be morbid. Neither I nor Orville wanted Gwen to continue full-time on the *Gazette* after they were married. If she was disappointed that I did not urge her to, she did not mention it.

My reason was simple to me. I felt that the time would come soon when I would want her at the office and he would want her elsewhere and she would be torn between the two of us. To me the paper was the most important thing in the world. While she never felt quite that way about it, she had enjoyed it, and had worked loyally, efficiently, and creatively. After October 31, 1937, though, her first consideration would have to be Orville, their own lives, and their business. Years later she would remind me wryly that she had not really been consulted about how she felt, and in retrospect that may have been true.

They had made their decision. To me it seemed unwise. I thought they should have waited, but that was beside the point. They had a right to an opportunity to work out their destinies without comment or interference on my part. I knew that if she were still on the *Gazette* I would interfere. I could not help it. If evening came and there was work to be done, I would expect her to do it along with me, regardless of their plans. Nor could I figure out any possible financial arrangement that would pay her what her time would be worth and would also be fair to me, since I always expected to work day and night.

I would miss the frequent features, and I hated the very thought of taking over her Spickard ads, but many of my own duties were requiring less time as I became more proficient. Long hours were of no concern to me. I still had many plans for the paper, and if I had to carry them out alone, that was the way it was. I thought most of my life probably would be spent doing things alone.

Gwen sometimes accused me of putting things ahead of people. I couldn't make her see that people get themselves into terrible predicaments and it worried me to death when I couldn't do anything to help them. They were unhappy in their jobs, or they lost their money, or they had love affairs with tragic endings and they told me all the details. Action always had been my own remedy for any trouble, whether it meant merely moving to a different room if my boarding place became unpleasant or making a more drastic change for a larger problem. The only things I couldn't take were uncertainty combined with doing nothing about a problem and prolonged indecision.

Action, hard work, constructive planning, and taking immediate steps to carry out at least a part of the plan—these were my solutions, but they were by their very nature useful only to me. I couldn't map out other people's paths and start them along a route I had set, one that probably would not be right for them. I could only listen, sympathize, and carry their burdens home with me to sleepless nights and anxious days.

Then, too, people let you down. You became attached to them. They died, got married, or moved away. There was no way I could explain that any apparent coldness or indifference on my part toward humanity was a matter of self-defense. To care too much, for me, was to be destroyed. Being alone had its disadvantages, its inconveniences. It had its compensations, too. If you guessed wrongly, at least you did not involve anyone else.

I made one resolve. All my life I had tried to look

after my little sister. Sometimes I hadn't done so well at it. There had been times when the things that worked for me didn't pan out for her. I had urged her to go to the University of Kansas, when she might have liked another school better. I had arranged for her to stay with friends of mine, to take courses I had liked, but the pattern that had suited me perfectly had not made her so completely happy. Perhaps she would have liked living in the residence hall, which I had not enjoyed. She did stick to her journalism major, however, which had paid off. She had not enjoyed a poetry class that had enchanted me.

From now on I would give no advice. If I didn't approve of what Gwen and Orville did, I would keep my comments to myself. My little sister had given me to understand she was quite grown up, and I would take her word for it.

That decision proved to be the wisest one I ever made. We had shared many happy experiences, but at times our associations had been marred by my tendency to dominate and my sharp words when she rebelled. My intentions were of the best, but whether from lack of understanding or lack of tact I had often failed. It was time for me to bow out. Perhaps we had both grown up.

I did not know it then, but out of our changed relationship there was to grow a better understanding than we had ever shared before—an acceptance of each other for what we were and are and a genuine enjoyment of the many things we had in common. I had lost my little sister, but in relinquishing the role of elder sister I had gained a forever friend.

Chapter 16

The Gazette Goes On

Ardis

Spickard accepted Gwen's marriage without surprise. In fact, it acted as though that was just what it had expected all along, and it took quite in stride my regular appearances on her ad beats. To my astonishment I didn't lose a single advertiser, and while I never learned to relish that part of the work, I did get it down to a system so that it took as little time as possible.

Because Orville had discovered a special talent and liking for printing, it was logical that he run the job department. He was able to combine the extra work with his own business and to figure each job to include payment for his time and expertise with a profit to cover use of the *Gazette* equipment. Gwen contributed features and occasional news stories under her byline, and I was surprised how smoothly the transition was made.

We divided our furniture and sold the pieces neither of us wanted, and I moved into a large second-floor room at the home of the Fred Hopper family in one of

Gazette Goes More *Streamline* with Addition of New Type

New type and equipment to continue the "streamlining" of the paper begun two years ago were purchased by the Grundy County Gazette this week.

This publication of the Gazette appears with a new heading in open-face Stymie, a modern type, new modern Stymie headline type, a modernized second deck and a modernized version of its feature headings. New type to be used in advertisements in which a modern form of typography is especially desirable also has been added.

For the purpose of facilitating the work in the mechanical department the Gazette is buying an electric saw which will make the cutting of metal in the back shop more true and less difficult than it was with a hand saw.

New modern job type was added to the job printing department of the Gazette early this spring, and the modern design of printing for letterheads, envelopes, circulars, and other kinds of printing for which distinction is desirable has proved exceedingly popular with the Gazette's customers. C. Orville Thogmartin, who has made a special study of printing in connection with his own mail order business and who has been manager of the Gazette's job printing department for the past fifteen months, has done the designing for the job department and has offered valuable assistance with the planning of the "streamlined" paper.

Modern form of printing is characterized by simplicity. In job work this is accomplished by the squaring the lines, the use of modern type faces, the elimination of all unnecessary symbols or decoration and the employment of dots, triangles, or squares when emphasis is needed. On the modern letterhead the printing is likely to be done with the lines set f

(directly under each other) rather than pyramided. Fancy borders are seldom used.

Similarly, readability and simplicity characterize the "streamlined" paper. Headings are set in caps and lower case instead of all caps because that practice makes them more readable. The lines of the heading are flush instead of "staggered" or pyramided for the same reason and also because when the flush headings are used the headline may be written to suit the contents of the story rather than to obtain lines that are exactly the same length whether they have much meaning or not.

Modern type faces are plain and readable rather than fancy and obscure. Two of the types added to the job department, "modern tourist" and "airport," suggest by their names the present day trend of economy, efficiency and speed which [...] modern printing as well [...]

The [...] Misso [...] "stre [...] as [...] foll [...] mo [...] we [...] pl [...] tw [...] te [...] h [...]

* * * * * * * * * * * * *
* Maybe this is sticking our *
* necks out, but we're asking *
* for it and really want your *
* opinion. *
* Do you like the new *
* streamlined make-up of the *
* paper, and if so, why? Or, *
* if not, why? *
* For the best criticism, for *
* or against, written out and *
* sent or handed to the Ga- *
* zette editor, not less than *
* twenty-five nor more than *
* than fifty words long, the *
* Gazette will give one year's *
* subscription. For the second *
* best, six months subscrip- *
* tion. For the third, three *
* months. You don't need to *
* know anything about news- *
* papers to write the best crit- *
* itism. Just tell why in your *
* own words you do or don't *
* like the new make-up and *
* appearance of the Gazette. *
* Or if you don't want to *
* write it, tell us anyway. We *
* want to know! *
* * * * * * * * * * * * *

the older mansions. It provided a pleasant view of the setting sun from a huge bay window and had a good-size closet that I used as a kitchenette. The Hoppers, a devoted couple in their early forties, made me more than comfortable in their happy home. They had four daughters, two who, though quite young, were already married, a third in high school, and the youngest in grade school. Fred's mother lived with them as well; although blind, she took an alert interest in whatever was going on.

A couple of years earlier the *Gazette* had reported that the Hoppers also had a son, which left the editors, then new in town, with very red faces. During the frozen winter of 1936 we hired a local boy to pick up locals and help around the shop. Hank Selser, a brother-in-law of Fred Hopper's, thought it would be a great practical joke to give him that item. Not knowing the Hoppers at that time, we let it go by. Kes thought it a bit strange but, unusual for Kes when he suspected something wrong, said nothing. A son in a family of four daughters would have been quite an event. When the item came out in the paper, Fred's mother, then living in Kansas City, spent a dollar on a telephone call to see if it was true.

The Hoppers, good sports that they were, just laughed about the error, especially when they found out that Hank, who ran the local café, was the instigator. Hank introduced himself to strangers as Hank Selser, adding, "I have two brothers, Alka and Bromo." Gwen felt vindicated for the joke Hank had played on us and the Hoppers when, one day as she was eating her lunch at the café—a hamburger and a cup of coffee that cost five cents each—a customer came in with his own sandwich and asked for ketchup and a glass of water.

Mrs. Hopper was a wonderful cook, and when I arrived home late after an afternoon in Trenton she would often call me into the kitchen for a generous helping of roast beef with potatoes and gravy, leftovers to them, but to me a full meal of the kind I did not attempt to cook for myself with my limited equipment and relish for the art of cooking. They taught me to play simple card games such as rummy. If they wanted to spend an evening with friends or at a movie, I would take a book to read and sit with the youngest daughter and her grandmother to relieve the Hoppers of any hesitancy they might have felt about leaving them alone. It was small pay for those "leftover" meals.

In the spring, however, the Hoppers moved to Princeton to be nearer his work as superintendent of a construction project, so after a few mutually unsatisfactory months with the next tenants of the house as my landlords, I rented the two front rooms of a cottage on the hill in the east part of town. With more energy than skill I nailed wallboard across the opening between these rooms and the remainder of the house, which was to be occupied by another family. The partition gave me an apartment with the front porch and front entrance. The other people used a side door. In many of the houses in Spickard there were often no doors between rooms. Gwen and I wondered if the carpenters had never heard of doors. Of course in a house with small rooms a large opening between two rooms gave a feeling of space. Living and dining rooms often were combined in that way.

The large room I arranged as a living room-kitchenette, while the north room became a closet and in winter a refrigerator. Not trying to use and heat it simplified the fuel problem. Having no intention of ever attempting to make fires again, I sent to a mail-order house for a kerosene circulating heater with a cover that could be lifted to protect the wall behind the stove and expose burners for cooking. For a dollar I bought wallpaper at a close-out sale for the entire room, and for another dollar— her usual charge—a Spickard woman hung it. Being in the chips—1938 was an election year—I treated myself to new drapes and a studio couch; thus, with my book-case and books, I was pleasantly situated. Dad's Christ-mas check meant a small radio, and I even bargained with a Trenton furniture dealer to swap advertising for a good used piano so that Gwen could have one, too, since neither of us wanted to be without. Gwen had thought that since I was the sister who had pursued the most advanced study on piano while she had taken violin and voice lessons also, the original piano should be mine.

The 1938 election campaign meant more than a new studio couch. I bought a portable typewriter to replace the wreck that was wearing a permanent ache between my shoulder blades and established a savings account labeled in my mind "car fund" against the time when my old reliable Nancy would probably fall apart like the wonderful one-horse shay.

The election profits meant also new type for the *Gazette*. We had already adopted a streamlined makeup and were eager for some new typefaces to enhance it. Orville, who had studied every available trade magazine on printing and typography, every newspaper and mag-azine he could find, and every piece of printing he saw, helped us select them. We carried a front-page story modestly calling attention to the improvements we were continuing to make and boldly adopted the slogan, "Northwest Missouri's Most Modern Weekly." Gwen thought up the slogan, and it did apply, at least typo-graphically. The *Kansas City Journal* had become stream-lined just a few weeks before, but it wasn't a weekly.

The campaign also meant, for me, a wider acquaintance over the county and the cementing of friendships started two years previously through common political interests. Grundy County Republicans made it a point to offer strong candidates for local offices, people they could be proud to support. When we urged, "Vote the straight Republican ticket," we wanted to know that everyone on that ticket was worthy of such backing, and it was one of my greatest thrills to be behind the scenes with a small group of leaders who discussed whom we could get to run for what and mapped the plans for various meetings.

In August the Republican Women's Club selected Agnes Mae Wilson, a Trenton lawyer, as president and, to divide the honors among the three towns of the county, named me vice president and a Galt woman secretary. Since I made several trips a week to Trenton and since Charlie Schooler of Spickard was chairman of the party's central committee, with which we worked closely, the arrangement was a convenient one, allowing me to help to coordinate the activities of the two groups.

Agnes, a brilliant person who had served a term as prosecuting attorney (she was the only Republican elected in the landslide of 1932 when even Grundy County went Democratic), was a tireless worker, and under her leadership our club became the largest Republican women's organization in the state with fifteen hundred members. As an appointee of Forrest C. Donnell when he was governor, she later served a six-year term (1943–1949) as a member of the Missouri Public Service Commission, the first woman to hold that position.

Another of my best friends was Mary McRae, whose boss, George Mapes, was running for reelection as county clerk. Since his race was uncontested, George needed to make no campaign speeches in his own behalf and was given the job of explaining at the various meetings held in different parts of the county the several consti- tutional amendments, on which, naturally, the party did not take sides. One of these was Amendment Seven, a hodgepodge that, he said, "had everything in it." Mary, who between working, caring for aged parents, and go- ing to political meetings, hadn't time to keep her room in order, dubbed it "amendment seven" and made me welcome there whenever I didn't feel inclined to drive back to Spickard alone late at night.

Spickard was proud of the *Gazette*'s part in the cam- paign, and our activities helped to extend our influ- ence and make the paper count in the community. I was pleased, too, when at the November 1938 press meeting in St. Louis, the *Gazette*, to my immense surprise, was awarded first place for the best news story in a statewide contest sponsored by Missouri Press Women and when, two years later, it won recognition for news, editorials, and feature stories in similar contests.

The Missouri Press Women organization was a source of great inspiration and pleasure to me and a basis for the formation of lasting friendships with a number of the state's outstanding newspaper women long after I had sold the *Gazette*. After I left Spickard I spent a year as managing editor for a firm publishing a daily and two weekly newspapers in northern Illinois, and then I returned to Missouri and resumed my contact with news- paper friends from all over the state. With men being drafted into military service and women working in high- paying munitions factories, teachers had become scarce. My contribution to the war effort was to teach English and journalism in a consolidated high school about fifteen miles south of downtown Kansas City. My journalism class learned about story construction, accuracy, responsibility, deadlines, and writing.

After the war I bought a house in Kansas City in an era when few single women bought houses or lived alone. My positions in journalism included four years as editor of the *Kansas City Realtor*, a weekly published by the Real Estate Board, then an all-male institution. The only discrimination I experienced was in pay. I attended meetings of the Missouri Press Women for many years, retaining my membership until I moved to Emporia in 1990.

Marriage was not a part of my plan; when it came, I was probably as surprised as anyone. Charles Etem, a school board member when I taught during World War II, was owner of an insurance agency. Our acquaintance was renewed when I phoned him to write a policy on my house. His wife had died, and his son, Charles, Jr., was a salesman for the agency. When Charles and I married in 1951, he made me a partner, active in the business, which doubled the first year. Our time was cut short by his death in 1953. The business was then mine, but my stepson and I continued as partners as my husband had wished. Later, Charles, Jr., purchased the business in installments. Once the transfer of ownership was completed in 1970, I took early retirement. Our cordial and rewarding relationship lasted until his death in 1993.

Dr. Roy Anderson and I met at a speaker's club of Dale Carnegie alumni. We married in 1958. We traveled extensively, often doing what we enjoyed most, dancing. He died in 1981.

Chapter 17

Ethel

Ardis

I first knew Ethel as a slender, dark-haired woman who combed the Spickard streets gathering news for our rival paper, the *Missourian*. That was at the beginning of our experience as editors when Gwen was doing the local beat.

Soon they hit upon the novel plan of taking opposite sides of the streets and meeting at our office to swap items. "Why not?" they asked. "We'd both get the same items anyhow. This saves a lot of work." They were always careful to write the stuff up differently and change the order so McGuire would not catch on.

Ethel was the breadwinner for her family. Arthur, her tall, good-looking husband, although fully recovered from an eight-year fight against tuberculosis that had kept him in the sanatorium at Mount Vernon for some time, had been left with a heart condition that made steady employment impossible. He worked when he was able. When a house on the east edge of Spickard was put up for sale to settle an estate, they borrowed the money to buy it, and he did what he could around the place and looked after their son, Wendell, while Ethel worked harder than ever to support them and pay off the mortgage.

Ethel had a fine sense of humor, intelligent gray eyes above high cheekbones, a style her clean, mended clothing cast off by a more fortunate sister could not disguise, and more courage than anyone else I have ever met. She took in washing at seventy-five cents to a dollar for a family laundry. She worked in the canning factory in season. She gathered news and sold subscriptions for the *Missourian*. She sold cosmetics for a firm specializing in house-to-house canvassing for orders. She kept her chin up.

When I, too, moved to the east side of town in the summer of 1938, she was my nearest neighbor; after Arthur's death left her alone, we spent a great deal of time together. She knew the country roads and the country people. Sometimes we would drive out to look for feature stories and pick up subscriptions for cash or exchange. Occasionally we would get more than we asked for—one time I had to chase a huge Rhode Island Red rooster all over the back seat of Nancy when he escaped from the gunny sack the farmer's wife had put him in for us to carry him home. Ethel dressed and cooked the rooster, and we shared a scrumptious but simple meal.

Meeting stiff competition, she was elected tax collector for the township, and we worked out an arrangement for her to have a desk in the *Gazette* office. She continued to take in washing; every dollar was needed to finish paying for her house and the funeral bill.

We were both night owls, I from long habit dating back to college days when I stayed up late to study in the quiet after my housemates had retired, she from long necessity of so many undertakings to carry on. Often in winter evenings, hours after Spickard had rolled up the sidewalks and turned in, I would bundle a coat over my pajamas and robe, tie a scarf over my head, pull on overshoes, and with a flashlight—standard equipment in that town since streets were poorly lighted—slip across the back way to chat with her while she ironed.

Her intelligence and high ambition to live graciously showed through her poverty in everything she did. She still played the piano on Sunday afternoons. She managed to read current magazines and papers. She kept her repainted linoleum highly polished. Her house was as neat and clean as the shirts beneath her swiftly moving iron. Her fire was warm, her hospitality never-failing. If you dropped in at noon and she and Wendell were having lunch, you had to share it even if it was only bread and gravy and cold milk from her Jersey cow. Sometimes that was all there was, but it was always good.

Ethel always saw the humorous side of things, and the joke was frequently on herself. She had never stopped learning. Married at nineteen, a reserved country school-teacher who had completed but two years of high school, all Spickard had offered at that time, she had been faced with the discovery of her husband's illness when she was scarcely recovered from a serious operation and with her son still a toddler. Her health had never been the best, but her spirit remained undaunted.

One evening she told me she had decided to finish high school. The superintendent of schools had agreed to arrange a study course by which she could complete her work and take examinations on the various subjects she would need. It meant having to study when she was already tired from a hard day's work, but she persisted until she obtained her diploma.

Some stories of the women who coped with adversity in the depression days did not have happy endings, but Ethel's did. The sequel came during World War II after I had moved away from Spickard. Rightfully it is not a part of the *Gazette* girls' story, I suppose, and yet it belongs here in that Ethel was such an inspiration with her strength and her companionship. Her story does have its minor note, for long years of worry and half-starvation took their toll, but I learned that there is still some justice in the world, so the story has a right to be told.

Wendell enlisted in the navy on his seventeenth birthday. To him, the navy meant getting away from Spickard with its lack of opportunity. A tall, too-thin youth, he was proud, highly sensitive, and ever conscious of his mother's struggle to shield him, her anxiety lest an early infection that had kept him in the sanatorium for two years as a preschool-age child might return, her too great effort to make up to him for things other children had that he lacked. Ethel signed his papers reluctantly, thankful that at least his acceptance for military service meant a clean bill of health.

During his training, he was sent to a radio school in the East and she went to visit him. En route home on the train she met a friend of Wendell's, a curly-haired lad named Don, also in the navy, on the way to visit his father, who had bought a farm near Mill Grove, a little town in the hills not far from Spickard. Because Ethel mothered all boys, Don, whose own mother had died when he was too young to remember her, instinctively told Ethel all about himself and the father who had reared him.

"I wish you could meet my dad," he declared when she got off the train.

Ethel had no desire to meet his father, although not

for the world would she have said so and hurt his feelings. As an attractive woman with an ailing husband and later as a widow, she had scrupulously avoided the attention of men, some of whom had not been too honorable in their intentions and some of whom had not been too desirable. There was a dearth of unattached desirable men in Spickard, and in any event she felt she should concentrate on Wendell and his welfare.

Don kept writing to his father about Ethel, and Don wrote Ethel, too. His father tried to meet her. She continued to find excuses to evade him. "All men are wolves," she had often said with just enough twinkle in her eye and her voice to rob the remark of harshness. She had no reason to assume Don's father was different.

Finally, he wrote her a letter in which he invited her to go to Trenton for a Sunday noon dinner and a movie. He would have to be home in time to do chores. Recalling a cryptic remark of mine from the past as to the security of broad daylight with plenty of people around, she accepted. He was not a wolf at all. He was of medium height with curly gray hair, kind eyes, and the big hands of a farmer who earned his living by hard work. Deeply religious, he was impressed with Ethel's high principles and the very fact that foremost in her mind was her devotion to rearing her son.

"He is so good," is the way she described him to me after they were married some time later. She had felt they should wait until the war's end, but he could see no reason for that. Both boys came home safely. After many years of caring for other people, Ethel finally had the most devoted care anyone could desire.

Chapter 18

"30" for the Gazette Girls

Gwen

Orville and I lived in an apartment in a wing of the home of his parents, Mort and Lera Thogmartin, for the first two years of our marriage, then moved our shop and all of the furniture we had salvaged from his and my collections of discards, plus a few pieces we had bought or received as gifts, to our first house. We rented a six-room house for the magnificent sum of $6.oo per month. When he first inquired of the owner what the rent would be, she said, "Well, I guess I'll just have to ask six dollars a month. I did rent it for five, but I had to have a lot of work done on it and I have to make some of that back."

She didn't object to our moving our press and cutter (we had acquired some larger equipment by then) into a back room from the small building Orville had built with the lumber from an old barn he had torn down. In spite of the fact that we were without running water or an inside bathroom, we felt pretty lucky and were proud of our new home.

I made a trip to Trenton in the secondhand Nash we had also acquired by that time and bought fabric for curtains and drapes. With a new linoleum rug, and plenty of wax and polishing, the house really looked quite cute. It had been redecorated inside, and we ignored the fact the floors sloped in all directions—most of the rentals in Spickard had similar faults, as Ardis and I had found.

Spring came in 1940 in Spickard, amazing us after the severity of the northwest Missouri winter. And in May spring was outdoing herself with an abundance of flowers, extra heavy foliage on the fine old trees, and just the right warmth for gardens. The day Ardis walked into my living room with her chin practically dragging down to her knees was as pretty a day as I ever saw, not at all in harmony with her woebegone expression.

"What on earth is wrong?" I asked in alarm before she had time to explain.

Her usually firm chin almost wobbled. "I've had a chance to sell the paper," she announced tragically.

"Well, goodness, sell it," I gasped in relief. "I thought it was something awful. We always planned to sell within a few years, and you and I know it has taught us about as much as it can."

"It's just like selling a member of the family," she mourned.

"Oh, gee whiz!" I exploded. For some reason her affection for possessions always aroused my impatience more than anything else, even though I knew she still did not especially care about their monetary value. "You actually feel worse about this than when you left home or I got married or anything like that."

"I know," she said with dramatic dignity, "but it has been my life for five years, and I don't know what to do without it." I refrained from reminding her that things didn't last forever any more than people did, which had been her reason for forming few close alliances.

"Well, it was our living but hardly our life," I conceded.

"Not yours," she acknowledged, "but it was mine."

It occurred to me that she was really serious and was feeling terribly sorry about the fact that the paper might be in hands that would not treat it with the tender loving care that hers had, so I stopped kidding and asked for details. We stood to make a nice profit, about a third more than we had paid originally, although, of course, we had built up the business and the equipment considerably. The price was, we felt, fair.

Ardis probably would have been content—as content as her nature would allow—to go on running the paper for years, but I urged her to sell it. For one thing, we saw the war clouds gathering on the horizon, and in some way I felt sure that sooner or later the problems of business in wartime would complicate our lives. I knew the probability that in the event war did come, Orville might not be around to help with buying and maintaining equipment, and the faithful Tavvy, being unmarried, would not be with her either. I could foresee real problems with help. Beyond that, I tried not to think.

Most of all, I felt that Ardis had reached the peak of anything Spickard or any small town had to offer her in the way of challenge and accomplishment. She had all the valuable experience that the past five years had brought her, and I felt she was wasting a lot of talent in not seeking larger fields. Also, I knew that when I left Spickard, which was inevitable eventually, since we, too, needed to broaden our business interests, Spickard would be a lonely place for her. There were few people her age and with her rather specialized interests. Young people were drifting away from the small towns as prosperity slowly returned. I could not have realized then that the needs of the military would draw so many away and that many small towns would in a few years become ghost towns. Who could tell which would survive?

I tried to explain all this to Ardis, and perhaps she recognized my logic was sound and not cluttered with the personal sense of loss that hers was, for she finally agreed to sell, although anything short of an amputation of her arm would have hurt her less, I think. When the details were all agreed to and the papers were signed, sealed, and delivered and we were no longer the *Gazette* girls, we took a little time for nostalgic reminiscing.

"It was fun while it lasted," I conceded, now that there was no danger of her changing her mind and keeping the paper after all. "It was a great experience and I wouldn't have missed it for the world."

"No, for at least five years of my life I can feel I was someone doing something," Ardis mused.

"You'll do a lot bigger and more important things than running a little country newspaper," I prophesied with a grin. "Your life isn't over. Why you are only twen- . . ."

"Shh!" Ardis commanded. "You know I never allow my age to be mentioned."

"OK, you're still young and you have a lot of good experience behind you. Now you are ready for something else worthwhile. You have the brains, education, personality, and experience. What else do you need?"

"I feel a hundred," Ardis admitted. "And I seem to have lost my sense of direction. I can't get organized."

But I was remembering. "It was a thrill the first time we printed ballots, wasn't it?" I recalled. "I didn't like working all night much after that, but that was our first really big printing job."

"I loved those all-night sessions," Ardis declared. "To me they were the most exhilarating and challenging experiences we ever had." I reflected to myself that she had forgotten how much she worried about whether or not we could meet our deadlines. But then I recalled that she said the things she hated most were getting up in the morning and going to bed at night.

"Remember the gallons of coffee you drank trying to keep awake?" she asked with a laugh. "And how the night owls and late loafers kept coming in to see what we were doing, and we kept hiding the coffee for fear someone would drink it and you couldn't stay awake without it?"

"Yes, every time we heard a footstep on the stair we whisked the coffeepot off the stove and under the desk, and the visitors would say 'I smell coffee.'"

"And you'd say, 'Gee, I wish I had some' so wistfully that they would have sworn there wasn't any within smelling distance," Ardis smiled.

"And remember that night I sat outside on the steps, one of those wonderful summer nights, waiting for the forms to be ready so I could feed press, and Frosty Watson and Kenny Fox and Kenneth Dickerson started harmonizing, and I sang with them for hours, every song we knew, I think. We gathered quite an audience before it was over. No one would have guessed it was depression time and kids were lucky to have two cents to rub together in their pockets, and probably none of us did." The remembrance was apropos of nothing at all, but that evening had become one of those rare jewels that come once in a lifetime with casual acquaintances when for a fleeting moment you feel close and happy.

"Remember the time I got up in a political meeting and ad-libbed a speech that went over like a tent, and

even told a joke that people laughed at—me!" Ardis
spoke with wonderment at such a rare occasion that she
smiled only after my giggle at her typical Ardisism.

"Well, they did," she insisted.

"Of course they did, dear," I soothed. "No one except you thought you were a flop."

"Remember the features we wrote, the people we
met, the ways we figured out how to handle people and
problems . . ."

"And the expression on your face the time the man
came in and said, 'I want to advertise my wife,'" Ardis
interrupted.

"Well, how was I to know she was running up a lot of
bills on him which he wanted to let people know he had
no intention of paying," I asked defensively if ungram-
matically.

"I wish I had a dollar for every time I rewrote the
country correspondence or every time I tried to be
original in saying, 'Mr. and Mrs. So and So and family
spent Sunday with her parents, Mr. and Mrs. Such and
Such,'" Ardis said. "I'll miss all that, even the monotonous little details."

"In a way, I suppose," I answered. "But it's the people
I'll miss, the wonderful, kind, funny, tragic human be-
ings that made it all so fascinating."

"I guess that was it for you," Ardis admitted, surprised that at last she understood what the paper meant
to me.

It wasn't just that I could have the satisfaction of
feeling that I might have had a bit of influence on the
issues of the community, or that our paper had helped
pass the street improvement bond, or that we had had a
hand in the elections by running stories about the candidates or printing the ballots, or even that many of my

features had been picked up by "Missouri Notes" in the *Kansas City Star.* The biggest thrill of the latter was not my accomplishment but the knowledge that Spickard residents enjoyed seeing the names of their neighbors and town in the big-city paper. It was a thrill when I had made someone happy because I had told the neighbors about their hobby, or the little triumph of growing the biggest tomato of the year, or a son's making the honor roll at college. I felt as though I had a finger on the pulse of humanity. The people were what it was all about.

There were never big or little people, just people. Of course there were some I didn't especially care for, but I cared about them. I can't say I never met a person I didn't like, but I can say I have met few who could not spark a little interest. The *Gazette* gave me the best "in" to people I could have had at a time in my life when I was finding out what interested me most. The personalities are what I'll remember forever.

Our friendly journalists to the north, the *Princeton Post,* told the story of the *Gazette*'s sale this way: "Ardis Hamilton, publisher of the *Grundy County Gazette,* a weekly published at Spickard, announced today the newspaper had been purchased by Howard W. Mills of Mound City. Mr. Mills will take charge of the paper at once." Our last issue was dated May 23, 1940, just seven weeks short of five years since our first issue. We were confident that Mr. Mills, who had started his newspaper career in 1909, would adhere to the standards we had set.

The *Princeton Post* story went on to review with generosity the improvements we had made and the honors we had received. We were gratified that many of the area newspapers carried similar stories. However, none of them could have told the complete story. To Ardis the paper was her baby, and she felt she was selling something near and dear to her.

As for me, I was at that moment more excited about a real baby, Orville's and my son, Clyde, who arrived on June 15, 1940. I was starting on another adventure. Orville and I would own another small paper later, then for many years return to his first love, printing, in our own shop. Eventually I would again have my opportunity to work with people when I took a job as the complex director of an eight-hundred-bed residence hall at Emporia State University in Emporia, Kansas. A staff of sixty student employees and the students and faculty I met as I finished my bachelor's degree provided lots of new people for me to meet. I am sure my experiences at Spickard, so long before, helped me handle that work. Later, I served as the administrative assistant at our local museum, and my experiences with people and with writing were a benefit there, also.

The day Clyde was five days old, Tavvy came to see us. How had I ever thought Tavvy unusually reserved. He fairly beamed at the baby and at us. We saw him often after Ardis left for a refresher course in journalism at the University of Missouri. She took a job as editor for a firm in Illinois that published a daily and two weeklies. Tavvy admitted the *Gazette* would never be the same after Ardis left.

The *Gazette* was getting along nicely without us, though, and while I was sorry that it seemed unlikely we sisters would ever share such an exciting experience together again, it was Ardis who missed it most. She liked her work, but she still felt lost without the *Gazette*.

"Being one of 'those editor girls' was the most interesting thing I'll ever do," she said sadly during one of her weekend visits. "And I'll probably go on telling people about it for the rest of my life."

"We can't have that," I said idly, "so we'll have to think up some other way of getting it out of your system."

Suddenly an idea struck me. "Hey," I exclaimed excitedly. "I know just the thing. I have a great idea. We could write a book!"

The light came back into Ardis's eyes and she began to smile. "You and your ideas," she said. "Here we go again."

"30" at the bottom of a news story told the printer that he had reached the end. It was time for "30" for the *Gazette* girls.

Epilogue

Gwen

How much the world has changed since the 1930s! Newspapers have changed, too. There were no op-ed pages in the thirties. Letters to the editors were seldom published in a regular column. If subscribers or readers wished to vent their wrath or express an opinion, they just barged into the office, usually on press day or when we were at our busiest, it seemed, and expressed verbally what was on their minds. It could be vitriolic or pleasing. We preferred the latter. Fortunately that was what we got most of the time.

Today, if a newspaper needed a photograph of a sweet potato or other garden triumph, it could reproduce one quickly with high-tech photography and printing methods. Lighting for inside pictures is no longer at the mercy of those dangerous flashguns that illumined by exploding powder.

Then, there were no computers with which to write,

spell check, seek the best word on a thesaurus, switch around paragraphs, and achieve other marvels of the electronic age. There were only those aging typewriters on which we battered out our stories. About the only thing the Hollywood movies got right about the newspaper business in the 1930s was the two-fingered method of typing, portrayed by a cigarette-smoking male reporter wearing a felt hat—indoors—that he tilted back on his head. I question whether anything except the two-fingered typing method was authentic. I never saw those Hollywood types in any of the many shops I visited, although they may have existed at the larger metropolitan papers. Fortunately, both Ardis and I typed. We looked things up in the dictionary, or at least she did. I did it more than she knew.

Computers also have put to rest cranky old metal-spitting Linotypes, which required tender loving care to keep them running and asbestos fingers for handling the hot slugs. They also eliminated the necessity of learning to read upside down and backwards. Linotypes had for the most part brought about the demise of hand typesetting in the 1930s, although most newspapers did still use hand-set type for advertising and headlines. Now newer technology has put the Linotype, too, to rest.

There were none of the high-speed offset presses that seem capable of spewing out endless streams of assembled and folded newspapers. There were only the counterparts of Old Bertha, who may have as her claim to fame having been the only press in existence to have spent a January night in an alley in below-zero weather. Old Bertha ruled the roost when she was turned on. She required accuracy. Woe unto the feeder who missed a sheet. The procedure then was to throw a big lever to stop her, roll the cylinder by hand, extract the torn sheet, sometimes in fragments, clean the printer's ink off everything, including hands, and start again. It was not a speedy process.

Assembling and folding papers by hand also took time. The Mustang mailer, a device that stamped the name and address of each subscriber from a previously cast slug, did not live up to its name for speed.

The speed of job presses depended on the dexterity of the feeder. The right hand fed the sale bill, envelope, letterhead, card, or whatever into the gauge pins on the platen, which tipped to meet the form inked by rollers that had picked up the ink from the ink plate and rolled it over the type in the form. The left hand snatched the printed page to remove it at about the same time the right hand was reaching for the next sheet of paper. Since the platen and the inked type form came together, a feeder who grabbed for a sheet that went astray could end up with a badly battered hand or fewer fingers. Ardis and I decided all those music lessons we had taken had taught us something besides how to play piano or violin; we had a sense of rhythm. I fed any of the presses, but Ardis firmly refused to endanger her small, pretty hands by feeding the job presses. In fact, she left the room when I fed them.

But there were those nights of sitting on the steps of the furniture store with other people my age joking about anything we found funny, and in those times so often bleak, it was surprising how much we found funny. Missourians love to tell stories, and it became a game to top each other. It was also the place I picked up a lot of my boxed features, and certainly the place I learned a lot about people. The future did not look too bright for many of us, but we had good humor and courage, and with the audacity of youth we all thought we could con-

quer our world. Many of us did. The prospect for today's youth is no doubt just as daunting—maybe more
so. Unfortunately, too many of my generation had their
dreams end with World War II.

Gone are the days when a fellow could take his girl to
a movie complete with popcorn and a hamburger and
soda afterward for a dollar. I am mystified at how young
people can afford today's high school proms with formal dress, tuxedo rental, corsages and boutonnieres,
and all the other expenses running into many times
more money for one night than we spent for a yearlong
courtship. In some places a limousine is an added expense. Maybe they have more fun than we did when we
rode four in the cab of John Earl's tank wagon when he
took out his girl, Lucille—and he filled up the tank wagon
with fuel for his filling station the next day before we went
for our movie-and-hamburger date—but I doubt it. Lucille and I, both widowed now, still keep in touch.

Life may have been simpler and less demanding then,
but we had to use imagination and creativity. Once, after
Orville and I were married, we entertained all sixteen
members of our card club on a $1.25 ham—that was the
price per ham, not per pound. Club members chipped
in about fifty cents each, and the guys built a ping-pong
table we used first for eating and then for playing. I
can't remember ever being bored.

There was the town baseball team, and wives and
girlfriends dutifully spent sweltering Sunday afternoons
cheering the Spickard team. I don't remember how often Spickard teams won. I remember we had a good
time. We could usually scrape up a nickel for a bottle of
pop. The profits from the pop went to buy baseballs;
admission to the games was free.

We had radio and listened to a Des Moines station

with a sports announcer named Ronald Reagan. There was lots of good music too, but we also enjoyed making our own music with those impromptu sing-alongs on the steps that were just made for sitting in front of several stores, thanks to a Main Street that ran uphill.

I can't imagine what a café owner would say now if someone came in with his own sandwich and asked for ketchup and water. I don't miss the brain sandwiches for five cents if you got tired of hamburgers. I learned something about cooking from the café cook. "How come your hamburgers always taste better than the ones I cook at home?" I asked.

"You probably wash your skillet with soap," she said seriously.

I hastily resolved not to eat hamburger there again, until I watched her clean her grill thoroughly with paper towels, a metal scraper, more towels, a quick rinse with boiling water and a thorough drying to prevent rust, then a quick heating, just to make sure. I received an iron Dutch oven for a wedding gift, and I still have it, thanks to the cleaning procedure she showed me. I also have those nonstick skillets that require special care as well.

One gentleman who had a steady job at the funeral home and furniture store was, I thought, extremely extravagant. He spent fifty cents a day for coffee. That bought ten cups. We didn't know about the health hazard of all that caffeine.

One night in 1939 Orville and I were driving home in our 1929 Nash from the famous Iowa State Fair in Des Moines. We had thrilled to the evening performance of Paul Whiteman and his orchestra and other wonders of the day. We stopped at Princeton to pour another quart of oil into the motor. That car used about equal quantities of oil and gas, but then we had paid only $75.00 for it. My husband came out of the filling station looking more sober than I had ever seen him. I suspected some car disaster. It was far worse than that.

"I just heard on the radio that Hitler has marched into Poland," he said.

It was the end of innocence. We held each other close, knowing that the world would never be the same.

Would I ever be one of the *Gazette* girls again? Sure, if I were twenty and the world was my oyster and the circumstances were right.

Would I want to go back to that time? Absolutely not. Not even to be young again.

I like writing with a computer. I like taking a plane to Europe in only twice the time it took for our first trip from Kansas to Spickard. I like having jillions of books to read and access to fine libraries, art galleries, museums. I like Pavorotti, Jessye Norman, the Boston Pops, and even the Oak Ridge Boys on television and compact disks. I like air-conditioned cars and houses, clean central heat, and automatic appliances, especially washers and dryers. No more carrying in buckets of water, heating them on a stove, and pushing the clothes in the washer with a lever to stir out the soil. No more hanging things on a line outside in every kind of weather, sometimes having to rush out and snatch them off before a rainstorm.

I like irons that have spray and steam, and I especially like wrinkle-free fabrics. I like sewing machines that make three hundred different stitches, and sergers that trim off seams. I like television, with its tons of information, even though I have a hard time sifting out reality from misinformation. High tech has more advantages than disadvantages, but it drives the world so rapidly that I, who grew up in the "kinder, gentler" world, sometimes want to cry, "Stop until I catch up." Nonetheless, I'm grateful for the ride. I like automatic transmissions in cars and four-lane superhighways.

I'm glad I didn't have to deal with some of the issues young people now face—drugs, crime, dangers we never dreamed of. In some ways, financially and physically, our lives were more difficult. In some ways they were easier. We didn't have to know so much. We could walk on the streets at night alone and be confident we were fairly safe. We have been asked if we experienced discrimination because we were female. Certainly we were very much aware of discrimination in many instances, especially when we were teaching for a lower salary than a man with the same job and qualifications would have received. On the *Gazette*, however, if we were discriminated against we did not notice it. I suppose as girl editors we were unique, but I never felt I sold an ad or subscription or job printing or did an interview any differently than a man would have done it or with less acceptance than a man would have received. Ardis was adamant that we not play on our youth or sex, and we never knowingly took advantage.

We have also been asked what sexual harassment was like at that time. We can speak only for small towns. We had never even heard the phrase, but there was opportunity for such harassment, certainly. It was probably easier to handle in a place where everybody knew everybody else, and gossip could spread like wildfire. I well remember the first time I went to the office of the superintendent of Spickard schools to set up a regular beat for a weekly column on school activities. The superintendent invited me into the office and closed the door, pulled a chair close to mine, and dropped his hand on my knee. I arose, opened the door, smiled at him, and inquired, "Would you prefer me to get the school news from the teachers or students?" I had been informed he liked seeing his name in the paper, and I wasn't above a little blackmail of that kind.

I left the door open, moved my chair away from his, and continued, "What activities are planned for this week?" The door was never closed again when I made my weekly visit. Other small incidents were handled much the same way. I think intimidation was easier then.

I'm glad I was young and had the experience of the 1930s era. It gave me a measuring tool, a scale on which to balance life. I always thought if we made it through the depression and the war of the early forties, we could make it any time, anywhere. Sometimes the years that followed took all the skills, the thrift, the knowledge the thirties had taught me. My first two years at the University of Kansas cost less than a thousand dollars. I didn't emerge with nearly as much knowledge as the students now who graduate with thousands of dollars of student loans to pay off, but I certainly had a lot of knowledge about the "real world," as it was designated by the students with whom I worked while employed at Emporia State University. And those students expressed the same apprehensions about their future employment that I had faced many years before.

I'm glad I saw it all. I'm glad we could tell about it. Every decade had its difficulties, its triumphs, its rewards, and, of course, its failures and sorrows. Even with today's opportunities, I would not want to do it again. Once around is a privilege. Now we can wish for today's and tomorrow's adventurers and young entrepreneurs just as good a time and experience.